Hello and welcome!

*Vor dir liegt der **Wordmaster**. Er hilft dir beim Wörterlernen.*

*Im Anschluss an die **New words** gibt es kurze Aufgaben, Rätsel und Wortspiele, mit denen du den neuen Wortschatz übst und festigst.*

*Sobald du neue Wörter in der Schule besprochen hast, bearbeite die **New words** in diesem Heft.*

*Die **fett gedruckten** deutschen Wörter sind Lernwörter. Sie fehlen im englischen Satz, damit du sie eintragen kannst.*

Alle Lösungen findest du auf dem beigefügten Lösungsblatt.

Unit 1

I love London

New words ▸ *pp. 8–9 | VOCABULARY p. 199*

1 Ein **Palast** ist ein großes Haus, in dem ein König oder eine **Königin** wohnt.	A ______________________ is a big house where a king or a ______________________ lives.
2 Wer ist Großbritanniens **Premierminister/in**?	Who is Britain's ______________________ ?
3 Wir lieben Fußball und gehen jeden Samstag ins **Stadion**.	We love football and go to the ______________ every Saturday.
4 Ich mag den Klang von Kirchen**glocken**.	I like the sound of church ______________ .
5 Der Kölner Dom hat zwei **Türme**.	Cologne Cathedral has two ______________ .
6 **Europa**	______________________
7 Köln ist berühmt für seinen **Karneval**.	Cologne is famous for its ______________ .
8 **Detektiv/in**	______________________
9 Viele Londoner fahren mit der **U-Bahn** zur Arbeit.	Many Londoners take ______________ to work.
10 Viele Großstädte haben eine **U-Bahn**.	Many cities have an ______________ .
11 Eine **Fahrt** mit dem London Eye ist teuer.	A __________ on the London Eye is expensive.
12 Ich gehe zu Fuß zur Schule; es **dauert** nur fünf Minuten.	I walk to school; it only ______________ five minutes.
13 Papa wird an Omas Geburtstag eine **Rede** halten.	Dad is going to give a ______________ at Grandma's birthday.
14 Wie **heißt** deine Schule?	What' __________ your school ______________ ?
15 Das **Parlament** ist eines der vielen Londoner **Sehenswürdigkeiten**.	The Houses of ______________ are one of the many London ______________ .

1 Lost words

Füge das richtige Wort in die Sätze ein.
Verwende die Wörter aus den Luftballons.

1 The Queen lives _______ Buckingham Palace.

2 A lot of Londoners go to work _______ the Tube.

3 How much did you pay _______ the shoes?

4 How long did you stay _______ London?

5 Did you enjoy your ride _______ the London Eye?

6 We travelled to France _______ our summer holidays.

7 France is famous _______ its good food.

8 Let's meet _______ the bus station _______ six o'clock.

9 How long does the bus ride _______ the stadium take?

New words ▸ *p. 10 | VOCABULARY p. 199*

1 Dylan arbeitet an der **örtlichen** Schule.	Dylan works at the _______ school.
2 *Harry Potter* wurde **von** J. K. Rowling geschrieben.	*Harry Potter* was written _______ J. K. Rowling.
3 Jim will Radio**reporter** werden.	Jim wants to become a radio _______.
4 **Ich wohne hier schon mein ganzes Leben lang.**	_______
5 Ich war schon einmal in Berlin, aber sonst **nirgendwo**.	I've been to Berlin once but _______ else.
6 In London gibt es viele **Dinge, die man tun kann**.	There are lots of _______ in London.
7 Die **Kehrseite** einer Großstadt ist der Lärm. Der **Vorteil** ist, dass man viel machen kann.	The _______ of a city is the noise. The _______ is that you can do lots of things.
8 Mama **kann** mir in vielen Fächern **helfen**.	Mum _______ me with lots of subjects.

New words ▸ *pp. 10–11 | VOCABULARY p. 200*

1 Wasch dich, du bist ganz **schmutzig**!	Get washed, you're very ________________.
2 Viele Mädchen interessieren sich für **Mode**.	Lots of girls are interested in ________________.
3 In unserem **Einkaufszentrum** gibt es alles.	You can get everything in our ________________.
4 Wir **kaufen** meistens auf dem Markt ein.	We usually ________________ at the market.
5 Meine große Schwester **darf** in die Disco **gehen**, ich nicht.	My older sister ________________ to the disco, I'm not.
6 In London gibt es viele verschiedene **Kulturen**.	In London there are many different ________________.
7 Kostas ist **Grieche**, Sean ist **Ire** und ich bin **aus Schottland**.	Kostas is ________________, Sean is ________________ and I'm ________________.
8 Der Unterschied zwischen meinem alten Dorf und dieser Stadt ist **riesig**.	There's a ________________ difference between my old village and this town.
9 Mein Bus ist abends immer **überfüllt** und auf den Straßen ist viel mehr **Verkehr**.	My bus is always ________________ in the evening and there's a lot more ________________ in the streets.

2 Word pairs

Ergänze die passenden Wörter.

French			
France	Scotland	Ireland	Greece

3 Crossword

Trage die Wörter in das Rätselgitter ein.

(11)

(4)

(5)

(7)

(1)

2 trendy way of dressing
3 very big
6 interesting things in a town that tourists visit
8 something or someone from Scotland
9 opposite of "clean"
10 cars, buses, bikes and people moving in a town

4 Odd word out

Unterstreiche das Wort, das nicht in die Reihe passt.

1 big – huge – tall – famous
2 car – bike – traffic – bus
3 fashion – amazing – great – fantastic
4 palace – tower – castle – detective
5 Greek – Irish – Scottish – English
6 train – underground – the Tube – boat

5 Spot the mistakes

In jedem Satz sind zwei Fehler. Unterstreiche und korrigiere sie.

1 Quien Elizabeth lives at Buckingham Palast. ______

2 Sherlock Holmes is a faimous dedective. ______

3 What's spezial about the London undergraund? ______

4 Can we wisit the Houses of Parlament? ______

5 Their were lots of people in the Tube. ______

New words ▸ *pp. 12–13 | VOCABULARY pp. 200–201*

1 Ich möchte gerne einen Tisch **reservieren**.	I'd like to ______ a table.
2 Was kostet eine **Tagesfahrkarte** in London?	How much is a ______?
3 Ich habe **nur** £5.	I ______ have £5.
4 Hast du den **Stand** mit den lustigen Hüten gesehen?	Have you seen the ______ with the funny hats?
5 Die **Olympischen Spiele** haben 2012 in London stattgefunden.	The ______ took place in London in 2012.
6 Die meisten Modegeschäfte sind an der **Hauptstraße**.	Most fashion shops are on the ______.
7 An meiner Schule gibt es **über** 500 Schüler.	There are ______ 500 students at my school.
8 Müssen wir darüber **diskutieren**?	Do we have to ______ this?
9 **Schreib auf**, was du davon hältst.	______ what you think about it.
10 Wir brauchen noch ein paar gute **Bildunterschriften** für unser Poster.	We still need some good ______ for our poster.
11 Wir müssen das Poster morgen der Klasse **präsentieren**.	We have to ______ the poster to our class tomorrow.
12 Haben wir schon eine gute **Überschrift**?	Do we have a good ______?

New words ▸ *pp. 14–16 | VOCABULARY p. 201*

1 Wir haben schon lange keinen **Kontakt** mehr.	We haven't had ____________ for a long time.
2 Unser Café liegt **abseits** des Touristen**pfads**.	Our cafe is ________ the tourist ________.
3 **Klick auf „Buchung"**, wenn du an der Tour teilnehmen möchtest.	____________ "____________" if you want to take part in our tour.
4 Einige **Kommentare** zu diesem Text sind sehr interessant.	Some ____________ on this text are very interesting.
5 Wie **häufig** fahren die Busse zum Bahnhof?	How ________ are the buses to the station?
6 Unser **Reiseleiter** kannte den **Weg** sehr gut.	Our ________ knew the ________ very well.
7 Darf ich auf Jans Party gehen? – **Auf keinen Fall**!	Can I go to Jan's party? – ____________ ____________!
8 Ich muss mich **ausruhen**.	I need to ____________.
9 Samstags treffen meine Freunde und ich uns im örtlichen **Jugend**club.	My friends and I meet at the local ________ club on Saturdays.
10 Meine Mutter hasst **laute** Musik.	My mother hates ____________ music.
11 Ich **bezahle** das Eis.	I'll ____________ the ice cream.
12 Auf den **Rolltreppen** in den Londoner U-Bahnstationen sollte man rechts stehen.	One should stand on the right on the ________ ________ in the London Tube stations.
13 Es hat lange gedauert, den neuen Berliner **Flughafen** zu bauen.	It took a long time to build the new Berlin ____________.
14 Neue **Ankunftszeit**: 8 Uhr.	New ____________ time: 8 am.
15 Herr Dix, bitte kommen Sie zum **Abflug-steig** 5.	Mr Dix, please come to ____________ 5.
16 Hattest du einen schönen **Flug**?	Did you have a nice ____________?
17 Wir sind mit einem großen **Flugzeug** geflogen.	We came on a big ____________.
18 Wir mussten eine Stunde am **Check-in** warten, bevor wir **einchecken** konnten.	We had to wait for an hour at the ________ before we were able to ____________.

6 What are the words: *think – think of – think about?*

Setze das richtige Wort in die Sätze ein.

1 Hi Tom, what do you ______________________ joining the football club with me?

2 Good idea, John. I'll ______________________ it.

3 I have to ask my parents first, but I ______________________ they will agree.

4 I like our new PE teacher. What do you ______________________ him?

5 I ______________________ he's great and he knows a lot about football.

6 You're right. I couldn't ______________________ a better PE teacher.

7 Bits and pieces

Verbinde die Silben, um englische Wörter zu bilden. Übersetze diese dann ins Deutsche.

1 under	side	______________	5 up	in	______________
2 down	ion	______________	6 trans	ator	______________
3 traf	ground	______________	7 check	port	______________
4 fash	fic	______________	8 escal	side	______________

8 Word building

Sieh dir die Wortpaare an und übersetze sie.

	Noun	German translation	Verb	German translation
0	ride	Fahrt; Fahrgeschäft	ride	reiten; fahren
1	speech		speak	
2	reporter		report	
3	shop		shop	
4	booking		book	
5	discussion		discuss	
6	presentation		present	

New words ▸ *p. 17 | VOCABULARY pp. 201–202*

1 **viel Aufhebens**	______________________
2 Wie können wir das Problem **lösen**?	How can we ______________ that problem?
3 Das **Naturkunde**museum in London ist fantastisch.	London's ______________ Museum is fantastic.
4 Der letzte **Dinosaurier** lebte vor ungefähr 65 Millionen Jahren.	The last ______________ lived about 65 million years ago.
5 Meine Mutter **rollte** mit den Augen, als sie meine schmutzigen Schuhe sah.	Mum ______________ her eyes when she saw my dirty shoes.
6 **So** ist es immer.	It's always ______________.
7 Wir müssen Toms Geburtstagsparty **planen**.	We have to ______________ Tom's birthday party.
8 **Reg dich nicht auf.**	______________________.
9 Wo müssen wir **umsteigen**?	Where do we have to ______________ trains?
10 Bitte **steigt** in den Bus ein.	Please ______________ the bus.
11 Wir müssen eine Bahn **in Richtung Osten** nehmen.	We have to take an ______________ train.
12 Covent Garden liegt an der Piccadilly **Linie**.	Covent Garden is on the Piccadilly ______________.

9 Opposites

Finde das Gegenteil.

1 very small	◂▸ ______________	6 calm	◂▸ ______________
2 arrival	◂▸ ______________	7 under	◂▸ ______________
3 upside	◂▸ ______________	8 old age	◂▸ ______________
4 not ... anywhere	◂▸ ______________	9 loud	◂▸ ______________
5 clean	◂▸ ______________	10 westbound	◂▸ ______________

New words ▸ *pp. 18–19 | VOCABULARY pp. 202–203*

1 Jen möchte ihr Auto **verkaufen**.	Jen wants to ________________ her car.
2 Das ist **typisch** für dich!	That's ________________ of you!
3 Können wir ein bisschen **umher**gehen?	Can we walk ________________ a bit?
4 Der neue Bahnhof kostet 20 **Millionen** Dollar.	The new station costs 20 ________ dollars.
5 Mein Hund beißt nicht; er ist **ruhig**.	My dog doesn't bite: he's ________________.
6 Nicht **berühren**!	Don't ________________!
7 Auf dem Schild steht „**privat**" – da dürfen wir nicht hineingehen.	The sign says "________________" – we're not allowed to go in there.
8 Uh, eine **tote** Ratte.	Oh, a ________________ rat.
9 Er ist Museums**wärter**.	He is a museum ________________.
10 **Fang** mich, wenn du kannst.	________________ me if you can!
11 Ich möchte gerne meinen **Standpunkt** erklären.	I'd like to explain my ________________.

10 The fourth word

Ergänze das fehlende Wort.

1 man – woman	king – ________________
2 cinema – ticket	the Tube – ________________
3 train – station	________________ – airport
4 just – only	noisy – ________________
5 bell – tower	football – ________________
6 shop – shop	speak – ________________
7 prime minister – Parliament	king – ________________
8 high street – shops	market – ________________
9 no people – empty	lots of people – ________________
10 picture – caption	text – ________________

11 Word snake

Übersetze die Wörter aus der Schlange und trage sie in das Rätselgitter ein. Wie heißt das Lösungswort?

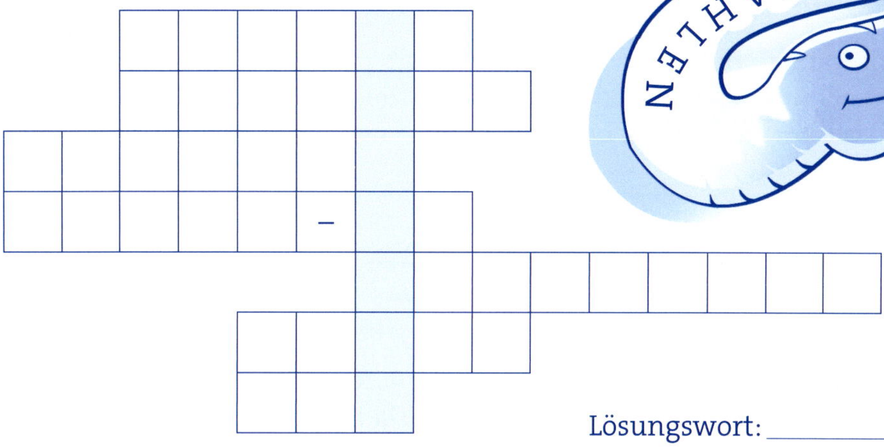

Lösungswort: ____________________

New words ▸ *pp. 20–21 | VOCABULARY p. 203*

1 Meine Oma macht einen Computer**kurs**.	My grandma is taking a computer ____________.
2 Ich schreibe jeden Monat einen **Artikel** für unsere Schülerzeitung.	I write an ____________ for our school magazine every month.
3 **Kilometer pro Stunde**	____________
4 Es kostet 5 Euro **pro** Person?	That's 5 euros ____________ person.
5 Mein Vater arbeitet in einem **Hotel**, meine Mutter in einem **Büro**.	My father works in a ____________, my mother in an ____________.

New words ▸ *pp. 22–23 | VOCABULARY p. 203*

1 Der **öffentliche Personenverkehr** in London ist großartig.	_______________ is great in London.
2 Das ist ein **öffentlicher** Strand.	This is a _______________ beach.
3 Tim ist erst **einmal** in England gewesen.	Tim has only been to England _______________.
4 Unser Hotel liegt in der **Stadtmitte** Londons.	Our hotel is in _______________ London.
5 Dafür brauchst du eine Fahrkarte der **Zone** 1.	You need a ticket for _______________ 1.
6 Was machst du **heute Abend**?	What are you doing _______________?
7 Wir gehen in den **Zirkus**.	We're going to the _______________.
8 Wir gehen runter zum **Damm**.	We're going down to the _______________.
9 Besichtige die St. Pauls **Kathedrale**!	Visit St. Paul's _______________!
10 Ich habe einen neuen **Klingelton** auf meinem Handy.	I have a new _______________ on my mobile.

12 Word search

Suche 9 weitere Verben im simple past *und schreiben sie in die mittlere Spalte der Liste. Ergänze dann links den Infinitiv und rechts das* past participle. *Du musst in vier Richtungen suchen: → ↓ ← ↙.*

A	S	L	P	A	I	D
R	B	E	T	S	P	M
L	E	F	H	T	F	E
Z	G	T	O	O	K	A
S	A	M	U	O	T	N
A	N	G	G	D	E	T
W	H	Y	H	R	E	W
T	O	G	T	E	U	I

	Infinitive	Simple past	Past participle
1	pay	paid	paid
2			
3			
4			
5			
6			
7			
8			
9			

13 Do you remember?

Du hast in dieser Unit neue Wörter zu den Wortfeldern „Dinge in der Stadt" und „Verkehrsmittel" gelernt. Kreise diese und weitere Wörter dazu im Buchstabenquadrat ein und schreibe sie dann in die Mindmap. Du musst in sechs Richtungen suchen: → ↓ ↑ ← ↙ ↘.

P	S	F	I	R	E		S	T	A	T	I	O	N	H	S
O	U	T	B	U	A	I	R	P	O	R	T	A	O	B	H
S	P	U	U	N	Q	A	B	W	C	C	D	S	E	F	O
T	E	B	S	D	U	G	E	H	A	I	P	A	R	K	P
	R	E		E	A	R	B	F	J	I	K	L	M	N	P
O	M	M	S	R	R	S	E	R	T	A	E	H	T	O	I
F	A	U	T	G	I	C	P	A	I	Q	T	R	A	I	N
F	R	I	O	R	U	H	L	R	S	D	S	H	O	P	G
I	K	D	P	O	M	O	T	U	V	W	G	X	Y	Z	
C	E	A	Z	U	A	O	B	C	D	M	U	E	S	U	M
E	T	T	O	N	E	L	F	G	H	C	I	N	E	M	A
I	J	S	O	D	T	A	X	I	P	A	L	A	C	E	L
K	L	M	S	W	I	M	M	I	N	G		P	O	O	L
M	A	R	K	E	T	T	N	A	R	U	A	T	S	E	R
N	S	H	O	P	P	I	N	G		C	E	N	T	R	E

Country life

New words ▸ *pp. 29–31 | VOCABULARY pp. 203–204*

1 Wir wollen ein altes **Bauernhaus** kaufen.	We want to buy an old ______________.
2 In Deutschland muss man 16 sein, um einen **Traktor** fahren zu dürfen.	In Germany you have to be 16 to be allowed to drive a ______________.
3 Ein **traditionelles** Rezept	A ______________ recipe
4 Wohin gehst du? – **Nirgendwohin.**	Where are you going? – ______________.
5 Ich will nicht **am Ende der Welt** wohnen.	I don't want to live ______________.
6 Ich **versuche**, um 20 Uhr zu Hause **zu sein.**	I'll ______________ home at 8 pm.
7 Toms neues **Geschäft** ist in Oxford.	Tom's new ______________ is in Oxford.
8 Mein Bruder will auch **ein Geschäft aufmachen.**	My brother wants to ______________ ______________ too.
9 Papa hat einen **Lieferwagen** von Cem geborgt.	Dad borrowed a ______________ from Cem.
10 Wir wollen eine **Überwachungskamera** in unserem Garten **installieren.**	We want to ______________ a ______________ in our garden.
11 Ich habe so viele Hausaufgaben. **Es nervt!**	I have so much homework to do. ______________!
12 Könnte ich eine Pastete **oder so was** haben?	Could I please have a pasty ______________ like that?
13 Eine Reise nach Cornwall **hört sich** gut **an.**	A trip to Cornwall ______________ good.
14 Ich brauche den Ball nicht; du kannst ihn **behalten.**	I don't need the ball; you can ______________ it.
15 **Halt mich auf dem Laufenden!**	______________!
16 Oma hat oft **Schmerzen.**	Grandma is often in ______________.
17 Ich habe mein Handy verloren. **So ein Mist!**	I've lost my mobile. ______________!
18 Hunde müssen im Park an der **Leine** sein.	Dogs must be on a ______________ in the park.

1 What's the word: *anywhere, everywhere* or *nowhere*?

Setze das richtige Wort in die Sätze ein.

1 You have to be careful on the Dartmoor roads – there are sheep ____________________.

2 We've looked ____________ for our little dog, but we couldn't find him ____________.

3 Where have you put my book? – ____________________, I didn't have it.

4 Are you going ____________________ this summer? – No, we're staying at home.

New words ▸ *p. 32 | VOCABULARY pp. 204–205*

1 Tim ist ein **Held**.	Tim is a ____________________.
2 Er war sehr **mutig**, als er in den **tiefen** Fluss gestiegen ist.	He was very ____________ going into the ____________ river.
3 Jedes Jahr **ertrinken** viele Menschen, weil sie nicht schwimmen können.	Every year lots of people ____________ because they can't swim.
4 Bitte hilf mir, diese **schwere** Tasche nach oben zu bringen.	Please help me take this ____________ bag upstairs.
5 Sie sprang ins Wasser, um Charlie zu **retten**.	She jumped into the water to ________ Charlie.
6 Ich wusste nicht, wie ich **reagieren** sollte, als mich der Hund angriff.	I didn't know how to ____________ when the dog attacked me.
7 Lehrer **leisten** jeden Tag **großartige Arbeit**.	Teachers ____________ every day.
8 Unsere Hunde **jagen** immer Kaninchen.	Our dogs always ____________ rabbits.
9 Sam hat **in letzter Zeit** oft die Schule geschwänzt.	Sam has skived a lot ____________.
10 Hast du ein **aktuelles** Foto von ihm?	Do you have a ____________ photo of him?
11 **Polizeimeister** Cox	____________________ Cox
12 Du musst andere Leute **respektieren**.	You have to ____________ other people.
13 Ich habe großen **Respekt** für Ärzte.	I have a lot of ____________ for doctors.
14 Die **Landschaft** um Bremen ist sehr schön.	The ____________ around Bremen is very nice.
15 Weißt du **irgendetwas** über unsere neuen Nachbarn?	Do you know ____________ about our new neighbours?

New words ▸ *p. 33 | VOCABULARY p. 205*

1 Mia ist nicht zu Hause. Kann ich **ihr etwas ausrichten**?	Mia isn't at home. Can I ____________ ____________?
2 Die Müllers sind nicht zu Hause. Bitte **hinterlasst eine Nachricht** nach dem Ton.	The Müllers aren't at home. Please ____________ ____________ after the tone.
3 Hallo. **Hier spricht** John Smith.	Hi. ____________ John Smith.
4 Kann ich bitte **mit** Jana **sprechen**?	Can I ____________ Jana, please?
5 Ich suche rote Stiefel. – **Leider** haben wir **im Augenblick** gar keine Stiefel.	I'm looking for red boots. – ____________ we don't have any boots ____________.
6 Mein Bruder war **neulich** sehr krank.	My brother was very ill ____________.
7 Mia ist Herrn und Frau Browns Tochter, Miles ist ihr **Sohn**.	Mia is Mr and Mrs Brown's daughter, Miles is their ____________.

2 Numbers and letters

Zu jeder Zahl gehört ein Buchstabe. Finde zuerst die Lösungswörter. Vervollständige dann den Lösungssatz.

Dear Lucy,

The Cotswolds are nice, but I M I S S (1 2 3 3) you. Our house is in the middle of _ _ _ _ _ _ _ (4 5 6 7 8 9 8). There isn't even a _ _ _ _ (3 7 5 10) or a _ _ _ _ _ _ (13 7 11 9 13 7) here. But mum and dad's new _ _ _ _ _ _ _ _ (12 11 3 2 4 8 3 3) isn't far from here, so they drive me to school in our new _ _ _ (15 16 4). Then they go and _ _ _ _ _ _ _ (2 4 3 17 16 18 18) CCTV _ _ _ _ _ _ _ (13 16 1 8 9 16 3) on people's farms. After school I can't see my friends because they live too far away. It _ _ _ _ _ (3 11 13 19 3)! But – I have a dog now. He's called Rowdy. I have to keep him on a _ _ _ _ (18 8 16 21) when I go for walks with him so that he can't _ _ _ _ _ (13 7 16 3 8) the _ _ _ _ _ _ _ _ (1 2 18 18 2 5 4 3) of sheep that live here.

How are you? How is school? How are your new teachers? Any new classmates?

_ _ _ _ (19 8 8 10) _ _ (1 8) _ _ _ _ _ _ (10 5 3 17 8 21)!

Hope to see you soon.

Nadja

New words ▸ *pp. 34–36 | VOCABULARY pp. 205–206*

1 Hast du **schon einmal** Sushi probiert?	Have you __________ tried sushi?
2 **Bist du schon einmal in** Oxford **gewesen**?	__________ Oxford?
3 Wir müssen **umziehen**.	We have to __________.
4 Ich war schon **zweimal** in England.	I've been to England __________.
5 Oma war beim Arzt. Sie bekommt das **Ergebnis** nächste Woche.	Grandma was at the doctor's. She'll get the __________ next week.
6 Wir wohnen hier **seit zwei Monaten**.	We've lived here __________.
7 Wir haben **seit August** nach einem neuen Haus gesucht.	We've been looking for a new house __________.
8 Meine Eltern sind beide **Ingenieure**.	Both my parents are __________.
9 Sie wollten nicht **Landwirte** werden, **nachdem** sie die Schule beendet hatten.	They didn't want to become __________ __________ they left school.
10 In unserer **Kneipe** gibt es auch leckeres Essen.	You can get yummy food at our __________.
11 Der **Pfad** hinter unserem Haus führt zu einem kleinen Fluss.	The __________ behind our house leads to a small river.
12 Hinter unserem Haus ist ein kleiner **Wald**.	There's a little __________ behind our house.
13 Schreib die Ergebnisse in das **Diagramm**.	Write the results in the __________.
14 Meine Eltern **fahren** immer mit dem **Rad** zur Arbeit.	My parents always __________ to work.
15 Wir wollen nächstes Jahr eine Amerika**reise** machen.	We want to do a __________ of America next year.
16 Du musst an der **Kreuzung** links abbiegen.	You have to turn left at the __________.

3 Picture puzzle

Finde vier weitere Dinge.

1 van
2 __________
3 __________
4 __________
5 __________

4 Word snail

Übersetze die Wörter ins Englische. Trage die englischen Wörter in die Wortschnecke ein. Die Anfangsbuchstaben in der Schnecke helfen dir. Das Lösungswort findest du in den grauen Feldern.

Lösungswort: __________

5 Linking

Verbinde die richtigen Wörter und übersetze dann die Ausdrücke ins Deutsche.

1 It	easy.	______
2 CCTV	message	______
3 Keep me	message	______
4 What	day	______
5 Take it	sucks!	______
6 take a	called	______
7 leave a	house	______
8 the other	posted!	______
9 be	camera	______
10 move	a pain!	______

6 Plurals

Ergänze die Pluralformen.

	Singular	Plural
1	business	
2	hero	
3	point of view	
4	child	

	Singular	Plural
5	culture	
6	high street	
7	downside	
8	upside	

7 Find the right word: *since* or *for*?

Ergänze das passende Wort in den Sätzen.

1 Tom has lived in Mickleton ______ 2013.

2 Sheila has lived here ______ she was a little girl.

3 We moved to the Cotswolds in May, so I've only lived here ______ five months.

4 How long have you known your best friend? – ______ we were five.

5 How long have you been at this school? – ______ three years.

New words ▸ *p. 37 | VOCABULARY p. 206*

1 Ist Rob wirklich ein **Großstadtsnob**?	Is Rob really a ____________________?
2 Manchmal fühle ich mich wie ein **Landei**.	I sometimes feel like a ____________________.
3 Die Katze unserer Nachbarn springt immer **über** unseren **Zaun**.	Our neighbours' cat always jumps __________ our ______________.
4 Du hast ein **Loch** in deiner Jeans.	You have a ______________ in your jeans.
5 Bleib bitte **neben** mir.	Please stay ____________________ me.
6 Alle **lachten über** ihn, als er vom Stuhl fiel.	They all ______________ him when he fell off his chair.
7 Eine **Prinzessin** ist die Tochter eines Königs oder einer Königin, ein **Prinz** ist ihr Sohn.	A ______________ is a king's or a queen's daughter, a ______________ is their son.
8 Der Bauer **trieb** die Kühe in den Stall.	The farmer __________ the cows into the barn.
9 Meine Oma **kann gut mit** Kindern **umgehen**.	My grandmother ______________ children.
10 Sie **errötete**, als sie den ersten Preis gewann.	She ____________ when she won first prize.
11 Sarah **trainiert Hütehunde**.	Sarah ____________________.
12 Kai versteckte sich hinter einem **Busch**.	Kai hid behind a ____________________.
13 Sie können hier nicht Ihren Müll **abladen**! Sie müssen ihn zur **Deponie** bringen.	You can't ______________ your rubbish here! You have to take it to the ______________.

8 Definitions

Finde das beschriebene Wort.

1 A place where adults go for a drink or to meet their friends: ____________________

2 More often than once, less often than three times: ____________________

3 Where two roads meet: ____________________

4 A place with lots of trees: ____________________

5 Something the farmer puts around his fields so that the animals can't get out: ____________________

6 Something shop owners install so that they can see what's going on in their shop: ____________________

New words ▸ *p. 38 | VOCABULARY pp. 206–207*

1 Tiere füttern ist **verboten**.	Feeding the animals is __________.
2 Hat die Polizei den **Umweltsünder** gefunden?	Have the police found the __________ __________?
3 Ich **schlage** dir **vor**, dass du dir die CD bei mir zu Hause anhörst.	I __________ that you listen to the CD at my house.
4 **Biete** deinem Freund etwas zu trinken **an**.	__________ your friend something to drink.
5 Bauer Jim feiert jedes Jahr ein großes Fest auf seinem **Hof**.	Farmer Jim has a big party in his __________ every year.
6 Unser **Innenhof** ist zu klein dafür.	Our __________ is too small for something like that.
7 Wir **erschraken**, als eine **Fledermaus** in unser Zimmer flog.	We __________ when a __________ flew into our room.
8 Manche Leute sind sehr **ungeduldig**, wenn sie warten müssen.	Some people are very __________ when they have to wait.
9 Frau Schmidt ist eine sehr **geduldige** Lehrerin.	Mrs Schmidt is a very __________ teacher.

9 Word ladder

Gehe von oben nach unten und verändere bei jedem Wort nur einen Buchstaben.

1 fine Hi, Sally, how are you? – I'm ???, thanks. And you?

2 __________ I looked for you, but I didn't ??? you.

3 __________ What ??? of films do you like?

4 __________ Prince William might be ??? of England one day.

5 __________ Let's ??? the bell – maybe Tom is there.

6 __________ She has a wonderful voice. I love to hear her ???.

7 __________ I've never heard this ??? before.

8 __________ I'm tired, I've had a ??? day.

New words ▸ *p. 39 | VOCABULARY p. 207*

1 Ich **klopfte an** ihre Tür, aber sie hat nicht aufgemacht.	I ______________________ her door, but she didn't open.
2 **Polizisten** müssen eine Uniform tragen.	______________ have to wear a uniform.
3 Bitte **störe** mich nicht, ich arbeite.	Please don't ____________ me, I'm working.
4 Die Polizei soll **nach** Umweltsündern **Ausschau halten**.	The police should ________________ dumpers.
5 Du kannst hier nicht **parken**. Du bist kein **Anwohner**.	You can't ______________ your car here. You're not a ____________________.

10 Word families

Ergänze die passenden Nomen zu den angegebenen Verben und übersetze beide ins Deutsche.

	Verb	German translation	Noun	German translation
1	sound			
2	ride			
3	respect			
4	depart			
5	fly			
6	dump			
7	discuss			
8	mean			
9	react			
10	suggest			
11	book			
12	sell			

New words ▸ *pp. 40–41 | VOCABULARY p. 207*

1 Jack ist im **Vordergrund** des Fotos. Die Frau im **Hintergrund** ist seine Mutter.	Jack is in the ____________ of the photo. The woman in the ____________ is his mother.
2 Du musst mir nicht jede **Einzelheit** erzählen.	You don't have to tell me every ____________.
3 Denk daran, deinen Text zu **strukturieren**.	Remember to ____________ your text.
4 Sein neuer Film ist **toll**.	His new film is ____________.
5 Ein guter **Grund**, um ins Kino zu gehen.	A good ____________ to go to the cinema.
6 Ich kann **aus vielen Gründen** nicht zu Jim gehen. **Erstens** hat meine Oma Geburtstag, **zweitens** bin ich müde und **drittens** wohnt Jim zu weit weg.	I can't go to Jim's ____________. ____________ it's my grandma's birthday, ____________ I'm tired and ____________ Jim's house is too far away.
7 Wenn du Rad fährst, bist du **unabhängig vom** öffentlichen Nahverkehr.	If you go by bike, you 're ____________ ____________ public transport.
8 Camping ist ein **idealer** Urlaub für Kinder.	Camping is an ____________ holiday for children.
9 Im letzten **Abschnitt** findest du eine **allgemeine Aussage** zum Thema.	In the last ____________ you'll find a ____________ about the topic.

11 Word snake

Übersetze die Verben in der Schlange und trage ihren Infinitiv sowie das simple past *und das* past participle *in die Liste ein.*

	Infinitive	Simple past	Past participle
1	write	wrote	written
2			
3			
4			
5			
6			
7			
8			

New words ▸ *pp. 42–43 | VOCABULARY pp. 207–208*

1 Wir haben unseren Hund durch einen **Aushang** im Supermarkt gefunden.	We've found our dog through a ______ in the supermarket.
2 Mein **Opa** ist über 80.	My ______ is over 80.
3 Welche **Figur** in *Twilight* findest du am interessantesten?	Which *Twilight* ______ is the most interesting for you?
4 Ich freue mich schon auf die nächste **Episode** meiner Lieblingsserie.	I'm looking forward to the next ______ of my favourite series.

12 Do you remember?

Finde 15 weitere Familienbezeichnungen und stelle sie paarweise zusammen.

A	B	X	C	G	R	A	N	D	M	A
I	Z	S	O	N	C	O	U	S	I	N
G	G	T	U	N	C	L	E	M	O	G
B	R	D	S	I	S	T	E	R	S	R
R	A	A	I	J	T	X	Q	T	T	A
O	N	U	N	Z	E	W	S	J	E	N
T	D	G	N	D	P	H	A	C	P	D
H	M	H	M	U	F	O	U	F	M	A
E	O	T	O	S	A	A	N	A	O	D
R	T	E	T	A	T	U	T	T	T	O
J	H	R	H	F	H	I	L	H	H	P
F	E	H	E	Z	E	M	M	E	E	X
S	R	G	R	I	R	Z	Y	R	R	R

1 grandfather, ______

2 ______

3 ______

4 ______

5 ______

6 ______

7 ______

8 ______

Liverpool … the world in one city

New words ▸ pp. 50–51 | VOCABULARY p. 208

1 Kein **Zutritt** für Kinder unter 12.	No ________ for children under 12.
2 Viele Menschen sterben, weil sie kein sauberes Wasser haben – es ist eine **Katastrophe**.	Lots of people die because there is no clean water – it's a disaster.
3 Ich kenne ein gutes **chinesisches** Restaurant.	I know a good chinese restaurant.
4 **Nenne** fünf deutsche Flüsse.	________ five German rivers.
5 Ich wohne in einem lebhaften Stadtteil mit vielen Studenten und **Migranten**.	I live in a lively part of town with lots of students and migrants.
6 Hamburg ist die größte deutsche **Hafenstadt**.	Hamburg is the biggest German portcity.
7 Bis 1865 war die **Sklaverei** in den USA erlaubt.	slavery was allowed in the USA until 1865.
8 Jack arbeitet für eine **internationale** Firma.	Jack works for an international company.
9 Ich habe mein Handy verloren. Ich bin so ein **Dummkopf**.	I've lost my mobile. I'm such a Sla________.

1 Words with different meanings

Finde jeweils ein passendes englisches Wort für die beiden unterstrichenen deutschen Wörter.

1 Wir brauchen noch Brot. — need, must
Du musst fleißiger arbeiten. — ________

2 Verstehst du die Aussage des Films. — ________
Auf dem Anrufbeantworter ist eine Nachricht für dich. — ________

3 mit dem Auto fahren — drive
die Kühe in den Stall treiben — ________

4 ein Kind vor dem Ertrinken retten — save, save money
regelmäßig Geld sparen — ________

5 über einen Bach springen — jump,
vor Schreck zusammenzucken — ________

New words ▸ *pp. 52–53 | VOCABULARY p. 208*

1 Das war ziemlich **dumm** von mir.	That was a dumb thing to do.
2 Eine **Richtlinie** an unserer Schule verbietet Gewalt.	There is a "no-fighting-____________" at our school.
3 Mein Vater verkauft **Süßwaren** wie Schokolade und Kekse.	My father sells confectionary like chocolate and biscuits.
4 **Immer mehr** Schüler sind gegen Kämpfen auf dem Schulhof.	____________ students are against fighting in the schoolyard.
5 Unser Schulleiter **suspendiert** jeden, der sich nicht an die Schulregeln hält.	Our principal ____________ everybody who doesn't follow the school rules.
6 Unser Lehrer **konfisziert** unsere Handys, wenn wir sie im Unterricht benutzen.	Our teacher ____________ our mobiles when we use them in class.
7 **Mit freundlichen Grüßen** John Smith	____________ John Smith

2 Lost words

Füge das richtige Wort in die Sätze ein. Verwende die Wörter aus den Luftballons.

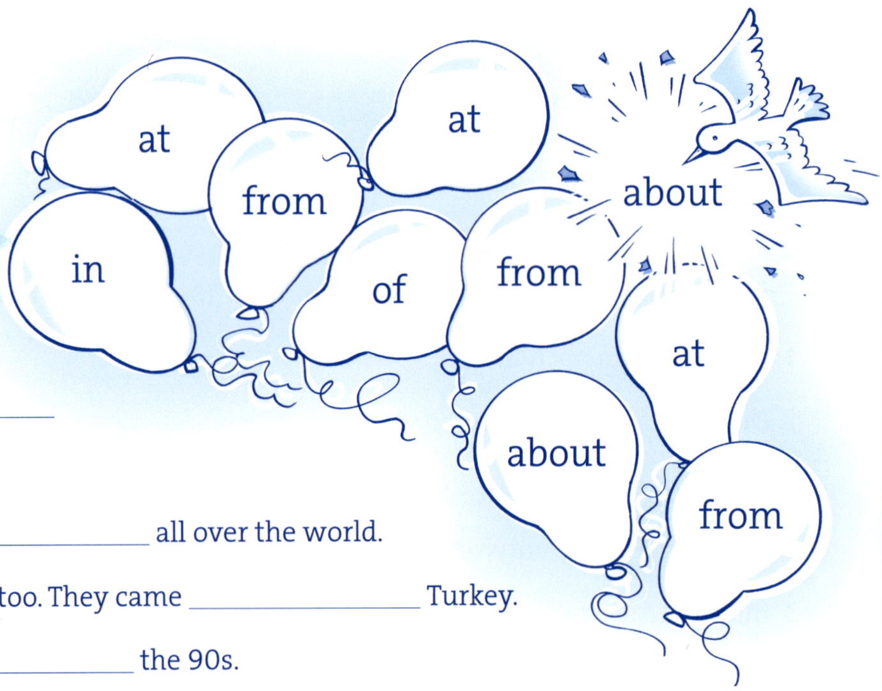

1 What's special about Cem's school?

2 Cem was very shy ____________ the beginning.

3 His new classmates came ____________ all over the world.

4 His own parents were migrants too. They came ____________ Turkey.

5 They had come to Berlin ____________ the 90s.

6 They spoke Turkish ____________ home, but German ____________ school.

7 Cem's school had a healthy eating policy. One day he had a packet ____________ crisps at school.

8 His teacher saw it and said, "I will send you home ____________ school if you do it again."

9 Cem felt very bad ____________ that.

New words ▸ *pp. 54–55 | VOCABULARY pp. 208–209*

1 Frau Schneider hat die **Begabung**, langweilige Themen interessant darzustellen.	Ms Schneider has a ______ for presenting boring stuff in an interesting way.
2 Meine Schwester ist gut in **Wirtschaftskunde**.	My sister is good at ______ ______.
3 Im letzten **Trimester** war ich sehr gut.	Last ______ I did very well.
4 Gibt es in diesem Geschäft einen **Verkäufer**?	Is there a ______ in this shop?
5 Hör auf damit! Ich meine es **ernst**.	Stop it. I'm ______.
6 Unsere Schule **nimmt an** einem Sport**wettkampf teil**.	Our school ______ a sports ______.
7 Olivia **ist gut in** Mathe.	Olivia ______ maths.
8 Französisch zu lernen ist eine neue **Herausforderung** für mich.	Learning French is a new ______ for me.
9 **Geschäftsleute** übernachten gerne in unserem Hotel.	______ like staying in our hotel.
10 Welche Art **Produkte** verkauft ihr?	What kind of ______ do you sell?
11 Beeilt euch – wir müssen **anfangen**!	Hurry up – we have to ______!
12 Ich möchte auch **Geld verdienen**.	I want to ______ too.
13 Das Geschäft meiner Eltern hat letztes Jahr einen großen **Gewinn** gemacht.	My parents' business made a huge ______ last year.
14 Dürfen wir hier **filmen**?	Are we allowed to ______ here?
15 Wir fahren zum **großen Finale** nach London.	We're going to London for the ______ ______.
16 Was **kostet** euer Schulessen?	How much does your school dinner ______?
17 Ich muss morgen ein **Referat** halten.	I have to give a ______ tomorrow.
18 Die Schuhe haben nur 30 **Euro** gekostet.	The shoes only cost 30 ______.
19 Möchtest du eine **Anstecknadel** oder einen **Ballon**?	Would you like a ______ or a ______?

3 Word building

Ergänze die beiden Tabellen. Vervollständige dann die Sätze mit einem passenden Wort aus den ausgefüllten Tabellen.

Noun			sale	plan	
Verb	enter	begin			rest

Noun	tradition	dirt		independence	
Adjective			national		challenging

1 Free ______________________ for children under five.

2 I need a ______________________ . I'm very tired.

3 Danger – don't ______________________ !

4 Please don't put your ______________________ shoes here.

5 We don't ______________________ sweets or crisps.

6 Mara is on the ______________________ hockey team now.

New words ▸ *pp. 56–58 | VOCABULARY pp. 209–210*

1 Kannst du mir etwas Geld **leihen**?	Can you ______________ me some money?
2 Die **Kokosnuss-Törtchen schmecken** gut.	The ______________________ nice.
3 Wir brauchen Brot. Ist hier in der Nähe eine **Bäckerei?**	We need some bread. Is there a ______________ around here?
4 Du musst jetzt **eine Entscheidung fällen**: Willst du das Auto kaufen?	You have to ______________________ : do you want to buy the car?
5 Wir haben die **Kekse selbst** gebacken.	We baked the ______________________ .
6 Auf der **Speisekarte** gibt es viele **Reis-gerichte**.	There are lots of ______________________ dishes on the ______________________ .
7 **Bienen** sind sehr wichtige Insekten.	______________ are very important insects.
8 Ich habe mich am Fuß verletzt – ich brauche etwas **Eis**.	I've hurt my foot – I need some ______________ .
9 Ich habe eine **Maus** als Haustier. Ich mag **Mäuse**.	I have a pet ______________________ . I like ______________________ .
10 Oma hat **Gurken** im Garten.	Grandma has ______________ in her garden.

4 Word partners

Verbinde die richtigen Partner, schreibe sie in die Liste und ergänze die deutsche Übersetzung.

1 air	ground		
2 inter	tone		
3 slav	graph		
4 ring	person		
5 country	ground		
6 cross	national		
7 fore	roads		
8 back	ery		
9 para	port		
10 sales	side		

5 Do you remember?

Du hast in dieser Unit neue Wörter zum Wortfeld „Essen und Trinken" gelernt. Suche 25 Wörter und schreibe sie in die passende Liste. Du musst in fünf Richtungen suchen: → ← ↓ ↘ ↙.

E	G	G	A	C	H	E	E	S	E	B	X	Y	F
C	Y	O	G	U	R	T	C	O	O	K	I	E	L
O	Q	M	L	C	H	O	C	O	L	A	T	E	O
C	P	E	B	U	T	T	E	R	S	N	Y	C	U
O	O	L	M	M	K	J	A	M	R	A	C	A	R
N	T	E	P	B	R	E	A	D	E	N	N	R	N
U	A	T	F	E	G	N	A	R	O	A	U	R	G
T	T	T	J	R	Y	T	S	A	P	K	T	O	C
B	O	E	Z	A	H	C	F	P	P	A	S	T	A
C	O	C	O	A	M	I	L	K	V	X	M	O	K
E	C	O	F	F	E	E	L	A	S	A	G	N	E

Fruits and vegetables	Things we get from animals	Things we make, cook or bake
cucumber,		

New words ▸ *pp. 59–61 | VOCABULARY pp. 210–211*

1 Die nächste **Tanzveranstaltung** an unserer Schule ist im August.	The next ______________ at our school is in August.
2 Die **Mischung** ist wichtig.	The ______________ is important.
3 Nimm nicht zu viel **Mehl**.	Don't use too much ______________.
4 Ich bin hingefallen und **habe** mir den Arm **gebrochen**.	I fell and ______________ my arm.
5 Mein Fahrrad ist schon wieder **kaputt**.	My bike is ______________ again.
6 Für ein Omelette braucht man **Eier**.	You need ______________ for an omelette.
7 Hör auf, alles auf den **Fußboden** zu werfen!	Stop throwing everything on the ______________!
8 Lecker! Ein Kuchen mit **Mandeln**.	Yummy! A cake with ______________.
9 Ich teile mir ein Auto mit meinem Bruder. **Es spart Kosten.**	I share a car with my brother. ______________.
10 Warum bist du **böse auf** mich?	Why are you ______________ me?
11 **China** ist ein riesiges Land.	______________ is a huge country.
12 Die Musik ist zu laut. Ich werde mich bei den Nachbarn **darüber beschweren**.	The music is too loud. I'm going to ______________ ______________ it to the neighbours.
13 Mein Bruder ist ein **erfolgreicher** Musiker.	My brother is a ______________ musician.
14 Er **muss** viel üben.	He ______________ practise a lot.
15 Was steht auf dem **Etikett**? – „**Leckere Sachen** aus der ganzen Welt."	What does it say on the ______________? – "______________ from all over the world."
16 Ich muss **testen**, ob mein MP3-Spieler funktioniert.	I have to ______________ my mp3 player to see if it works.
17 Ich **will, dass Tim** zu meiner Party **kommt**.	I ______________ to my party.
18 Meine Mutter hasst es, wenn ich meine Kleidung auf den Boden **werfe**.	My mother hates it when I ______________ my clothes on the floor.

6 Word web

Finde die Wörter, die in das Spinnennetz passen. Alle haben fünf Buchstaben und enden auf -e.

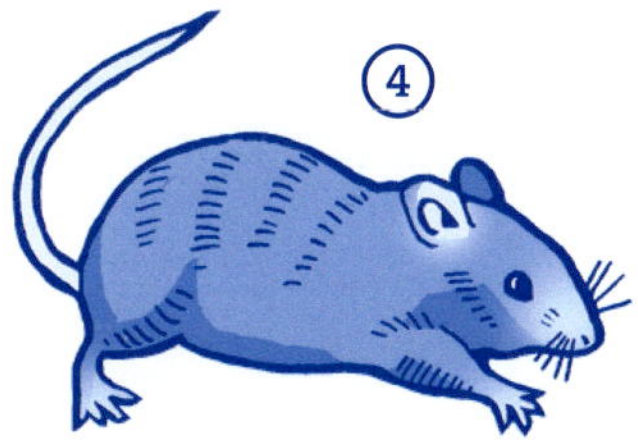

6 A present for the winner of a competition

7 What you do with your face when you're happy

7 Find the right word: *lend* or *borrow*

Setze die richtige Form von lend *oder* borrow *ein. Manchmal musst du auch eine Vergangenheitsform wählen.*

1 My bike is broken. Can I ________________ yours, please?

2 I forgot all my pens at home. – It doesn't matter, I can ________________ you one.

3 My brother never finds his swimming trunks, so he always wants to ________________ mine.

4 Tim ________________ me some money last week. I have to give it back to him tomorrow.

5 Oh, I never ________________ money from other people.

6 I ________________ a lot from my older sister when I was little.

New words ▸ *p. 62 | VOCABULARY p. 211*

1 Natasha Jonas ist eine britische **Sportlerin**.	Natasha Jonas is a British ______________.
2 Luc arbeitet **als** Tänzer.	Luc works ______________ a dancer.
3 An unserer Schule kann man **boxen** lernen.	You can learn to ______________ at our school.
4 Oma war die erste **weibliche** Person in unserem Dorf, die Auto fahren konnte.	Grandma was the first ______________ person to drive a car in our village.
5 Ich gucke mir die **olympischen Spiele** gerne im Fernsehen an.	I love watching ______________ ______________ on TV.
6 Ich freue mich, wenn unsere Sportlerinnen **Medaillen** gewinnen.	I'm happy when our sportswomen win ______________.
7 Natasha ist ein **Vorbild** für mich.	Natasha is a ______________ for me.
8 Ich glaube nicht, dass alle Männer **stark** und alle Frauen **schwach** sind.	I don't believe that all men are ______________ and all women are ______________.
9 Ich möchte fitter werden. Deshalb gehe ich jetzt zweimal die Woche in die **Sporthalle**.	I want to become fitter. That's why I go to the ______________ twice a week now.
10 Ich finde, man sollte ungesundes Essen **kennzeichnen**.	I think that one should ______________ unhealthy food.

8 The fourth word

Ergänze das fehlende Wort.

1 book – story	newspaper – ______________
2 heavy – box	______________ – question
3 somebody – nobody	somewhere – ______________
4 mother – father	daughter – ______________
5 horse – ride	bicycle – ______________
6 happy – unhappy	patient – ______________
7 text – paragraph	TV series – ______________
8 tomatoes and carrots – vegetables	chocolate and cookies – ______________

New words ▸ *p. 63 | VOCABULARY p. 211*

1 Ich finde Schuluniformen gut. Was ist deine **Meinung** dazu?	I think school uniforms are good. What's your ______________ on them?
2 Tom ist ein **fleißiger** Schüler.	Tom is a ______________ student.
3 Warst du krank? Du siehst so **mager** aus.	Have you been ill? You look very ______________.
4 Kannst du die **Aussage** dieses Liedes **zusammenfassen**?	Can you ______________ the ______________ of this song?
5 Bitte **fasst** den Text in 100 Wörtern **zusammen**.	Please ______________ the text in 100 words.
6 **Einerseits** finde ich das Internet toll, **andererseits** verschwende ich viel Zeit damit.	______________, I think the internet is great, ______________, I waste a lot of time on it.
7 Ich brauche bis Mittwoch eine **klare** Antwort.	I need a ______________ answer by Wednesday.
8 Im nächsten Trimester werde ich **auf jeden Fall** fleißiger arbeiten.	Next term I will ______________ work harder.
9 Ich werde **sogar** am Wochenende arbeiten.	I'll ______________ work at the weekend.
10 Ich hasse **gewalttätige** Menschen.	I hate ______________ people.
11 Nächstes Jahr **fange** ich **mit** Tennis **an**.	Next year I'll ______________ tennis.
12 Meine neue Schule ist gut, aber am **Anfang** fühlte ich mich etwas einsam.	My new school is good, but I felt a bit lonely at the ______________.

9 Opposites

Finde das Gegenteil.

1 in the end ◂▸ at the ______________

2 buy ◂▸ ______________

3 more and more ◂▸ ______________

4 be bad at sth. ◂▸ ______________

5 son ◂▸ ______________

6 over ◂▸ ______________

7 patient ◂▸ ______________

8 weak ◂▸ ______________

9 national ◂▸ ______________

10 grandma ◂▸ ______________

New words ▸ *pp. 64–65 | VOCABULARY pp. 211–212*

1 Lass uns ins **Fremdenverkehrsbüro** gehen und einen Stadtplan holen.	Let's go to the ______________________ to get a map.
2 Habe ich **erwähnt**, dass Jamie auch kommt?	Did I __________ that Jamie is coming too?
3 Jonas, **spiel ab**!	Jonas, __________________________!
4 Hamburg **besiegte** Stuttgart 3:1.	Hamburg _______________ Stuttgart 3:1.
5 Guter **Schuss**, Jonas!	Good ______________, Jonas!
6 **Pech gehabt**!	______________________________!
7 Deine **Zusammenfassung** braucht noch einen guten Schlusssatz.	Your ______________ needs a good phrase for the end.
8 **Seilspringen** und **Pilates** halten dich fit und gesund.	________________ and ___________ keep you fit and healthy.

10 Word families

Ergänze die Tabellen unten und vervollständige dann den deutschen Satz.

Noun	comment	name	notice	dump	
Verb					summarize

Noun	discovery		bicycle	film	
Verb		produce			answer

Manchmal haben englische Verben und Nomen ____________________________ Form.

Vervollständige die Sätze mit Wörtern aus den ausgefüllten Tabellen.

1 Please ____________________ the text in about 100 words.

2 Please ____________________ my question.

3 Don't ____________________ your rubbish here.

4 Visit our local museum. There are lots of things to ____________________.

5 Do you ____________________ to school, or do you go by bus?

11 Crossword

Trage die fehlenden Verben aus den Sätzen in das Rätselgitter ein.

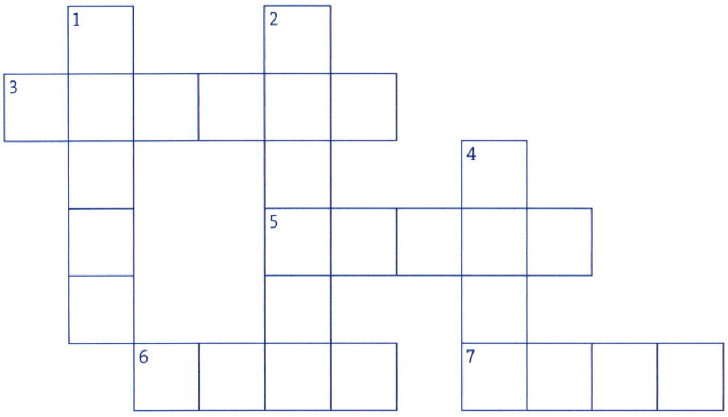

1 Tim fell and ??? his arm.
2 Hurrah, we've just ??? Munich 3:0!
3 Have you ever ??? a tractor? – No, I'm too young for that.
4 How much are the CDs? – They ??? £1.50 each.
5 Don't ??? these clothes away. Give them to the Oxfam shop.
6 John ??? me some money, and I have to give it back to him now.
7 We drove back in thick fog, so it ??? five hours to get home.

12 Word pairs

Welche Wörter passen zusammen?

take – be – get – make – make – sum – take – be

	started		money		part (in)		sth. up

	sth. up		good with		good at		a decision

Bonnie Scotland

New words ▸ *pp. 70–71 | VOCABULARY p. 212*

1 Das ist aber ein **hübscher** Hut.	That's a ______________ hat.
2 **Schottland** gehört zum **Vereinigten Königreich.**	______________ is part of ______________.
3 **das schottische Hochland**	______________
4 Berlin ist die **Hauptstadt** Deutschlands.	Berlin is the ______________ of Germany.
5 Der Joker ist Batmans **Feind**.	The Joker is Batman's ______________.
6 Ein rotes Herz ist das **Symbol** der Liebe.	A red heart is the ______________ of love.

1 Scrambled words

Die vermischten Buchstaben ergeben Wörter, die alle mit C beginnen. Die Übersetzungen und Zeichnungen helfen dir. Die Buchstaben in den grauen Feldern ergeben, von oben nach unten gelesen, die Lösungswörter.

_ _ _ _ _ _ _	LAACIPT	Hauptstadt
_ _ _ _ _ _	EEESHC	1
_ _ _ _ _ _	EATSCL	2
_ _ _ _ _ _ _ _	CCUUERMB	3
_ _ _ _ _ _ _	OOCNRTL	regulieren, bestimmen
_ _ _ _ _ _ _	CIRTHAY	Wohltätigkeit, wohltätige Zwecke
_ _ _ _ _ _ _	TENOMMC	Kommentar
_ _ _ _ _ _ _ _	ERIHCNDL	4
_ _ _ _ _ _ _	CCAUEKP	5
_ _ _ _ _ _ _ _	AIOCLPMN	sich beschweren/beklagen
_ _ _ _ _ _ _ _ _ _ _	DEUIOYTCNRS	Landschaft, Umgebung, Natur
_ _ _ _ _ _ _ _ _ _ _	EIIOOCNPTMT	Wettbewerb

2

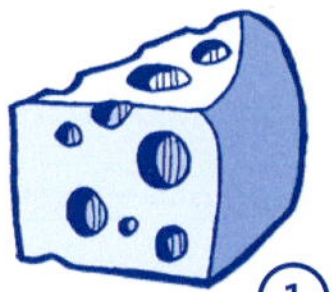
1

3

4

5

Lösung: _ _ _   _ _ _ _ _ _   _ _ _ G _ _ _

New words ▸ *pp. 72–73 | VOCABULARY pp. 212–213*

1 Bist du bereit für eine **Veränderung**?	Are you ready for a ____________?
2 Unser Buchladen muss **schließen**, weil zu viele Leute ihre Bücher online bestellen.	Our bookshop has to ____________ because too many people order their books online.
3 Tim hat eine gute Camping-**Ausrüstung**.	Tim has good camping ____________.
4 Wir haben kein Auto, also kaufen wir nie im Einkaufszentrum **außerhalb der Stadt** ein.	We don't have a car, so we never shop in an ____________ shopping centre.
5 Julia ist **Geschäftsführerin** einer Bank.	Julia is a bank ____________.
6 **Insgesamt** 30 **Arbeitnehmer** haben ihren Job verloren.	____________ 30 ____________ lost their jobs.
7 Alle von ihnen sind immer noch **arbeitslos**.	All of them are still ____________.
8 Warum **machst** du mir immer **Vorwürfe** wegen deiner schlechten Noten?	Why do you always ____________ me for your bad marks?
9 Freunde sollten **zusammenhalten**.	Friends should ____________.
10 Babys können sich nicht um **sich selbst** kümmern.	Babies can't look after ____________.
11 **Frühstückspension**	____________
12 Mein Vater weiß, **wie man ein Geschäft führt**.	My father knows ____________ ____________.
13 Frau Meyer **unterrichtet** Englisch.	Ms Meyer ____________ English.
14 In der Küche gibt es Kuchen. **Bedient euch**.	There is cake in the kitchen. ____________.
15 Ich arbeite in einem Outdoor-**Laden**.	I work in an outdoor ____________.
16 Ich werde mich bei der **Geschäftsführung** beschweren.	I'll complain to the ____________.
17 Unser Geschäft braucht mehr **Personal**.	Our business needs more ____________.

New words ▸ *pp. 74–75 | VOCABULARY pp. 213–214*

1 In unserer **Gegend** gibt es viele Seen.	There are lots of lakes in our ________________.
2 Tim, bitte **heiße** Oma **willkommen**.	Tim, please ________________ grandma.
3 Das Fluss**ufer** ist sehr hoch hier.	The river ________________ is very high here.
Da kann man nicht **fischen**.	You can't ________________ here.
4 Alle Getränke, **einschließlich** Tee und Kaffee, sind kostenlos.	All drinks, ________________ tea and coffee, are free.
5 Die Olympischen Spiele **finden** alle vier Jahre **statt**.	The Olympics ________________ every four years.
6 Ich möchte ein **Zweibettzimmer** buchen.	I'd like to book a ________________.
7 Wo kann ich meinen **Mantel trocknen**?	Where can I ____________ my ____________?
8 Was wollen wir Lily morgen **servieren**?	What do we want to ________________ Lily tomorrow?
9 **Esszimmer**	________________
10 **ein/e Sechzehnjährige/r**	________________
11 Oma hatte kein **Telefon**, als sie jung war.	Grandma didn't have a ________________ when she was young.
12 Ich möchte gerne meine **Reservierung** für den 18. November **bestätigen**.	I'd like to ________________ my ________________ for 18th November.
13 Unser erster **Gast** war **aus Kanada**.	Our first ____________ was ____________.
14 Bitte **ruf** deine Mutter **an**.	Please ________________ your mother.
15 Ich brauche ein **Messer**, um das Fleisch zu schneiden. Wo sind eure **Messer**?	I need a ________________ to cut the meat. Where are your ________________?
16 Was ist deine Lieblings**speise**?	What's your favourite ________________?
17 Äpfel und **Bananen** sind gesundes Obst.	Apples and ________________ are healthy fruits.

2 Find the right words

Setze myself, yourself, himself, herself, itself, ourselves, yourselves *oder* themselves *in die Sätze ein.*

1 I have to help grandma with this heavy box. She can't take it upstairs ____________.

2 When mum and dad are at work, we have to make dinner ____________.

3 Tim should ask ____________ why nobody wants to play with him.

4 Our neighbours' cat hurt ____________ when it jumped from the balcony.

5 How do you like my new dress? I made it ____________.

6 When I'm not at home, my children have to cook for ____________.

7 Ladies and gentlemen, food and drinks are in the kitchen – please help ____________.

8 Don't blame ____________. It isn't your fault.

3 Word ladder

Gehe von oben nach unten und verändere bei jedem Wort nur einen Buchstaben.

1 cost How much does the dress ??? ?

2 ________ It's cold outside; you need a ???.

3 ________ Can we go on a ??? trip on the River Thames?

4 ________ I always ??? my father at table tennis.

5 ________ Vegetarians don't eat ???.

6 meal This looks yummy. Enjoy your ???.

7 ________ I'll take the bike; it's a good ???.

8 ________ I've lost my school bag. – Oh ???!

9 ________ Please speak louder – I can't ??? you.

10 ________ Special equipment you need for sport or other things.

New words ▸ pp. 76–78 | VOCABULARY p. 214

1 **Bring** das Wasser **zum Kochen**, bevor du die Nudeln hinein tust.	____________ the water before you put the pasta in.
2 Kennst du berühmte **Schotten**?	Do you know any famous ____________?
3 Es spart Zeit, das Wasser im **Wasserkocher** zu kochen.	Boiling the water in the ____________ saves time.
4 Die **Kellner** und **Kellnerinnen** in unserem italienischen Restaurant sind sehr nett.	The ____________ and ____________ in our Italian restaurant are very nice.
5 Meine Schwester interessiert sich für technische Dinge. Sie will **Mechanikerin** werden.	My sister is interested in technical things. She wants to become a ____________.
6 Ich möchte **Empfangschef** in einer großen Firma werden.	I want to become a ____________ in a big company.
7 Wo kann ich mein Handy **aufladen**?	Where can I ____________ my mobile?

New words ▸ p. 79 | VOCABULARY p. 215

1 Wenn dir der Tee nicht süß genug ist, **füge** etwas Zucker **hinzu**.	If the tea isn't sweet enough for you, ____________ some sugar.
2 Du findest **Hinweise** dazu im Text.	You'll find some ____________ in the text.
3 Das Flugzeug **landet** in einer Stunde.	The plane will ____________ in one hour.
4 Wir haben kein Auto, aber wir **mieten** uns manchmal eines.	We don't have a car, but we ____________ one sometimes.
5 Du darfst ohne **Führerschein** nicht Auto fahren.	You aren't allowed to drive a car without a ____________.
6 Sie trat **auf** die Straße und einige Fahrer **hupten**.	She stepped ____________ the road and some drivers ____________.
7 **Glücklicherweise** ist nichts passiert.	____________ nothing happened.
8 Du siehst **gestresst** aus.	You look ____________.

4 Numbers and letters

Zu jeder Zahl gehört ein Buchstabe. Finde zuerst die Lösungswörter. Vervollständige dann den Lösungssatz.

Hi Julian,

I can't visit you this summer. We've had a few ___ ___ ___ ___ ___ ___ ___ (1 2 3 4 5 6 7) up here in the ___ ___ ___ ___ ___ ___ ___ ___ ___ (2 8 5 2 9 3 4 10 7). Three months ___ ___ ___ (3 5 11) dad lost his job because the last ___ ___ ___ ___ ___ (7 12 11 13 6) in our village had to ___ ___ ___ ___ ___ ___ ___ ___ ___ (1 9 11 7 6 10 11 14 4) because there weren't enough ___ ___ ___ ___ ___ ___ ___ ___ ___ (1 15 7 12 11 16 6 13 7). Now ___ ___ ___ ___ (17 11 12 2) my parents were ___ ___ ___ ___ ___ ___ ___ ___ ___ ___ (15 4 6 16 18 9 11 19 6 10). At first we were all shocked, but then mum had an idea, and last week we ___ ___ ___ ___ ___ ___ ___ (7 12 3 13 12 6 10) our own ___ ___ ___ (17 6 10) ___ ___ ___ ___ ___ ___ ___ ___ ___ ___ ___ ___ (3 4 10 17 13 6 3 21 20 3 7 12). We have to ___ ___ ___ ___ ___ (7 12 8 1 21) ___ ___ ___ ___ ___ ___ ___ ___ (12 11 5 6 12 2 6 13) now. Mum ___ ___ ___ ___ (13 15 4 7) the place, dad does all the ___ ___ ___ ___ ___ ___ ___ ___ (7 2 11 18 18 8 4 5) and I help after school. Our first ___ ___ ___ ___ ___ (5 15 6 7 12) was from Germany's ___ ___ ___ ___ ___ ___ ___ (1 3 18 8 12 3 9), Berlin.

I ___ ___ ___ ___ ___ ___ ___ ___ (14 6 9 1 11 16 6 10) her because I can speak a bit of German.

___ ___ ___ ___ (1 11 16 6) ___ ___ ___ (3 4 10) ___ ___ ___ ___ (7 12 3 19) ___ ___ ___ ___ (14 8 12 2) ___ ___ (15 7) ___ ___ ___ ___ (12 2 8 7)

___ ___ ___ ___ ___ ___ (7 15 16 16 6 13)!

Bye for now

Scott

5 Word friends

Zu jedem eingekreisten Wort passen zwei weitere Wörter. Verbinde sie mit dem eingekreisten Wort.

London employee buy king worker tent

capital **store** **staff**

palace **enemy** **equipment**

bad dangerous princess sleeping bag Berlin shop

New words ▸ *p. 80 | VOCABULARY p. 215*

1 Hier kommen wir nicht durch; die Straße ist zu **eng**.	We won't get through here; the road is too ______________.
2 Ich hasse **kurvenreiche** Straßen, weil mir in **Kurven** schlecht wird.	I hate ______________ roads because ______________ make me sick.
3 **Scheibenwischer**	______________
4 Ich konnte dich nicht anrufen, da wir keinen **Empfang** in den Bergen hatten.	I couldn't ring you because we had no ______________ in the mountains.
5 Unsere Schule ist ein sehr modernes **Gebäude**.	Our school is in a very modern ______________.
6 Mit welchem **Akzent** spricht er?	What ______________ does he have?
7 Ich **frage mich**, wann Emma kommt.	I ______________ when Emma will be here.
8 Die Geschichte handelt von einem Schloss, **in dem es spukt**.	The story is about a ______________ castle.
9 Venedig ist **so eine** hübsche Stadt!	Venice is ______________ nice city!
10 **Es gibt keine** Außerirdischen.	______________ aliens.
11 Du siehst verängstigt aus. Hast du ein **Gespenst** gesehen?	You look scared. Have you seen a ______________?
12 **Kanada** liegt in Nordamerika.	______________ is in North America.

6 Word families

Ergänze die passenden Nomen zu den angegebenen Verben und übersetze danach beides.

	Verb	German translation	Noun	German translation
1	change			
2	employ			
3	start			
4	store			
5	confirm			
6	reserve			

New words ▸ *p. 81 | VOCABULARY pp. 215–216*

1 Du kannst nicht bis **Mitternacht** aufbleiben.	You can't stay up till ____________.
2 Gestern **schien** den ganzen Tag die Sonne.	Yesterday the sun ____________ all day long.
3 Sean spielt **Dudelsack**.	Sean plays the ____________.
4 Bitte nicht auf die **Mauer** klettern.	Please don't climb on the ____________.
5 Er sah **verwirrt** aus.	He looked ____________.
6 Man hat fünf **Finger** an jeder Hand.	You have five ____________ on each hand.
7 Unser Geschäft ist auf der anderen Straßen**seite**.	Our store is on the other ____________ of the road.
8 Ist sie neu auf der Schule? – **Ich glaube ja**.	Is she new at this school? – ____________.
9 Ich kann ohne Probleme einen Marathon laufen. – **Das glaube ich nicht**.	I can run a marathon – no problem. – ____________.

7 Find the right words: time words

Setze die richtigen Zeitangaben in die Sätze ein. Der Kalender hilft dir dabei.

yesterday
last week
this Saturday
~~today~~
tonight
the night before
tomorrow

It's my brother's birthday *today*. My birthday was ____________.

We're celebrating with our friends ____________. ____________ our parents are cooking our favourite dish, haggis. Our grandparents arrived here ____________ and our oldest sister Holly came here ____________. She is going back to London ____________.

8 Opposites

Finde das Gegenteil.

1 ____________ ◂▸ employed

2 friend ◂▸ ____________

3 ____________ ◂▸ finish

4 full ◂▸ ____________

5 I think so. ◂▸ ____________

9 Plurals

Ergänze die Pluralformen.

	Singular	Plural
1	mouse	
2	16-year-old	
3	policy	
4	twin room	
5	employee	

	Singular	Plural
6	driving licence	
7	waitress	
8	knife	
9	enemy	
10	hero	

New words ▸ *pp. 82–83 | VOCABULARY p. 216*

1 **Stell dir vor**, du gewinnst eine Million Dollar.	____________ you won a million dollars.
2 Wir haben kein Auto, wir **reisen** immer mit der Bahn.	We don't have a car; we always ____________ by train.
3 Vor internationalen Fußballspielen hört man die **Nationalhymne** beider Länder.	You hear the ____________ of both countries before international football matches.
4 **Gott beschütze die Königin.**	____________.
5 Man konnte den **Stolz** in ihren Augen sehen, als sie den ersten Preis gewann.	You could see the ____________ in her eyes when she won first prize.
6 Mein Bein ist gebrochen; ich kann **mich** nicht **bewegen**.	My leg is broken; I can't ____________.
7 Unsere Wohnung kostet **tausend** Euro im Monat.	Our flat costs one ____________ euros a month.

10 Definitions

Trage die Wörter in das Rätsel ein. Wie lautet das Lösungswort in den grauen Feldern?

1 What you have to do with your mobile phone or mp3 player so that you can use them again
2 A chicken lays it
3 A popular Italian dish (it's not pizza!)
4 Not long ago
5 Another word for "call" or "phone" someone
6 Take food and drink to customers of a restaurant
7 The person who brings the customers their food and drink in a restaurant
8 Someone who comes to stay with you for a short time
9 The most important city of a country
10 Someone who works for a business
11 ◂▸ friend

Lösungswort: ______________________

11 Word building

Ergänze die Tabelle.

	Verb	Noun	Adjective
1		change	–
2	employ		
3	–	puzzle	
4		teacher	–
5	build		–
6	–		proud

New words ▸ *pp. 84–85 | VOCABULARY p. 216*

1 **Überfliege** den Text und suche nach **fett-gedruckten** Wörtern.	______ the text and look for words in ______.
2 Wir waren **ein paar** Tage in London.	We spent ______ days in London.
3 Ich möchte auch **irgendwo** hinfahren.	I want to go ______ too.
4 Wie war eure **Unterkunft** in Paris? – Schön. Wir hatten ein großes Zimmer.	How was your ______ in Paris? – Nice. We had a big room.
5 Wie lang war euer **Aufenthalt**? – Zwei Wochen.	How long was your ______? – Two weeks.
6 In Hostels gibt es meist nur **Schlafsäle**.	Hostels usually only have ______.
7 Du solltest jeden Tag eine warme **Mahlzeit** essen.	You should eat a hot ______ every day.
8 **Vielleicht** sollte ich kochen lernen.	______ I should learn to cook.

12 Find the right words

Übersetze die Verben ins Englische und ergänze die Formen in der Tabelle.

	German word	Infinitive	Simple past	Past participle
1	jmdn. unterrichten			
2	scheinen			
3	ein Hotel leiten			
4	zusammenhalten			
5	anrufen			
6	dauern			
7	schreiben			
8	bezahlen			
9	verkaufen			
10	fangen			

13 Word search

Kreise 30 Wörter ein, die du in Unit 1–4 gelernt hast.
Du musst in 6 Richtungen suchen: → ← ↓ ↑ ↘ ↙.

I	N	D	E	P	E	N	D	E	N	T	O	R	C	H	E
C	O	N	F	I	R	M	S	L	A	V	E	R	Y	Q	E
O	L	A	T	I	P	A	C	L	Y	U	A	C	U	G	M
A	K	N	I	F	E	M	A	B	C	M	R	I	U	V	P
T	B	A	N	A	N	A	T	M	A	O	P	H	D	S	L
C	S	E	R	I	O	U	S	Z	S	M	H	D	E	T	O
M	O	E	L	T	T	E	K	S	E	N	T	N	I	O	Y
W	B	U	O	B	I	N	R	N	D	O	U	I	C	R	E
B	A	T	N	H	G	O	T	H	W	L	C	B	E	E	E
A	B	S	G	T	A	B	R	E	T	S	A	S	I	D	K
O	L	O	M	D	R	I	R	O	T	A	L	A	C	S	E
N	Y	H	S	D	O	Y	T	A	T	O	M	I	G	E	N
T	D	G	E	Y	R	G	S	R	V	S	T	E	U	M	E
P	O	S	S	I	B	L	E	I	A	E	S	T	E	X	M
C	H	A	L	L	E	N	G	E	D	M	M	J	S	T	Y
S	H	O	T	I	M	P	A	T	I	E	N	T	T	Y	B

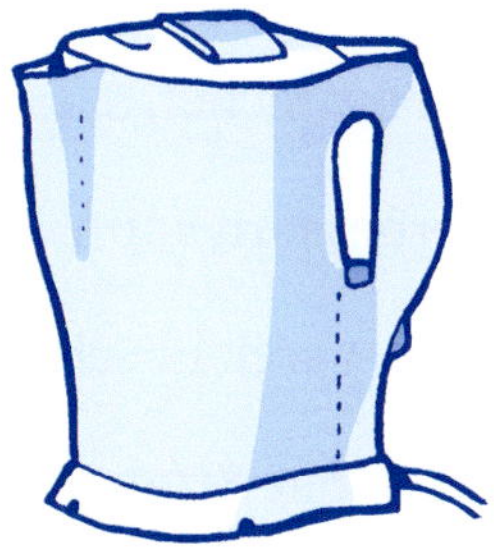

Words in German

Ausrüstung
Schuss
riesig
mutig
Hauptstadt
ruhig
ungeduldig
unabhängig
möglich
Gast
(Straßen-)Kreuzung

Scrambled words in English

yeeplome
eenmy
trycousinde
sterdisa
iousser
yaerslv
cghllnaee
aaabnn
resto
firmcon

A stay in Dublin

New words ▸ pp. 92–93 | VOCABULARY pp. 216–217

1 Ich möchte gerne an einem **Schüleraustausch** mit England teilnehmen.	I'd like to take part in an ____________ ____________ in England.
2 Ich bin sicher, dass ich dort mein Englisch **verbessern** kann.	I'm sure that I can ____________ my English there.
3 Wie war dein Schüleraustausch? – Es war eine tolle **Erfahrung**.	How was your school exchange? – It was a great ____________.
4 Ich mag Tee **lieber als** Cola.	I ____________ tea ____________ cola.
5 Wir fahren **wahrscheinlich** nach Dublin.	We're ____________ going to Dublin.
6 Ich möchte die Stadt gerne **kennenlernen**.	I'd like to ____________ the city.
7 **Es könnte sein**, dass ich mein Zuhause vermisse.	I ____________ miss home.
8 Die Straße war **teilweise** blockiert.	The road was ____________ blocked.
9 Was sind deine **Vorlieben** und **Abneigungen**?	What are your ____________ and ____________?

1 Word web

Finde die Wörter, die in das Spinnennetz passen. Alle haben fünf Buchstaben und enden auf -t.

①

3 This cathedral is beautiful. What a ???!
4 I'll pay for the meal. Be my ???.
5 My brother wants to ??? a business.
6 What enemies do
7 You get one ??? for each correct answer.

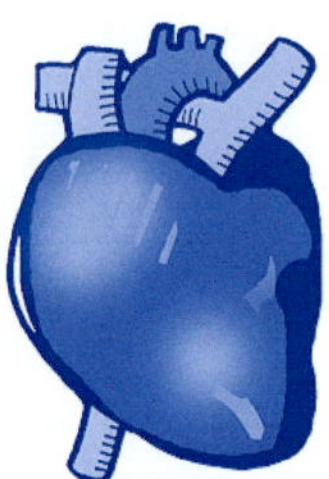
②

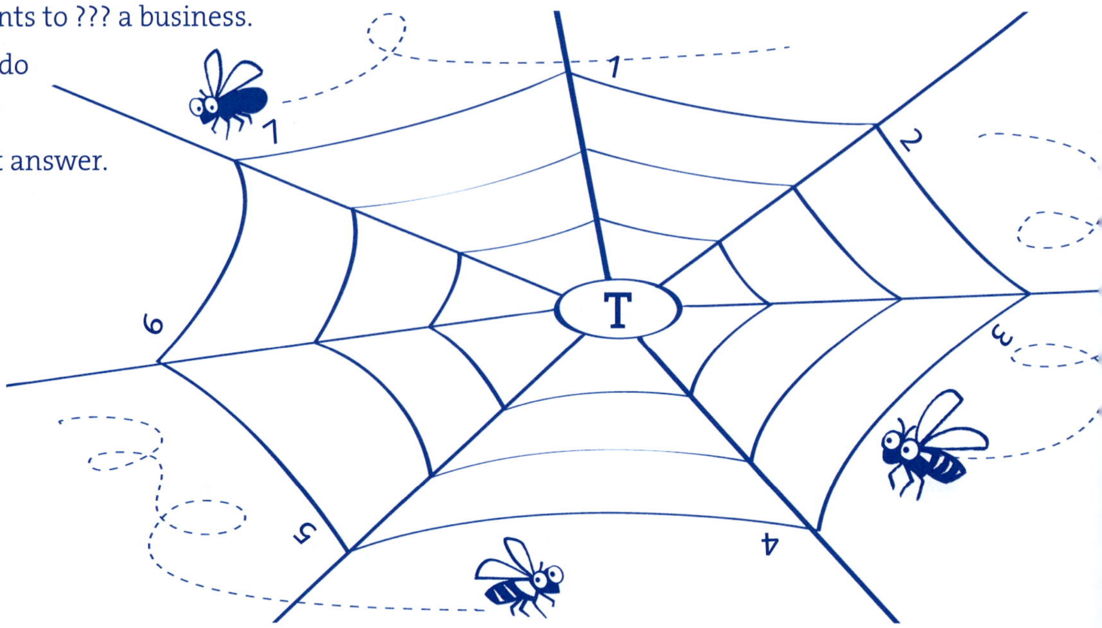

New words ▸ *pp. 94–95 | VOCABULARY p. 217*

1 Flug**nr.**	flight ______________
2 Auf welchem **Band** kommt unser Gepäck?	Which ______________ will our luggage be on?
3 Irland ist Teil der **EU**.	Ireland is part of the ______________.
4 Einwohner aus **Nicht**-EU-Ländern brauchen ein Visum.	______________ EU residents need a visa.
5 Ihr **Anschlussflug** nach Paris ist um 9 Uhr.	Your ______________ to Paris is at 9 am.
6 Hol dein **Gepäck** bei der **Gepäckausgabe** ab.	Pick up your ______________ at the ______________.
7 **Ausgang**	______________
8 Du darfst dein Handy nicht **während** des Fluges benutzen.	You mustn't use your mobile ______________ the flight.
9 **Reisepass**	______________
10 Ihr wart großartige **Gastgeber**.	You were fantastic ______________.
11 ein **ungewöhnlicher** Name	an ______________ name
12 **gewöhnlich**	______________
13 **Also**, können wir jetzt gehen?	______________, can we go now?

2 Find the right words: at the airport

Beschrifte die Zeichnung mit den englischen Wörtern.

New words ▸ *p. 96 | VOCABULARY pp. 217–218*

1 eine **Reihe** Häuser	a ______________ of houses
2 Ich **schüttelte** ihr **die Hand**. Sie **kicherte**.	I ________ her ________ . She __________ .
3 Meine kleine Schwester kann bis 20 **zählen**.	My little sister can ______________ to 20.
4 Karl war sehr **unhöflich** zu mir.	Karl was very ______________ to me.
5 Oma mag **Marzipan**.	Gran likes ______________ .
6 Sonntags gehen wir im **Wald** spazieren.	On Sundays we go for walks in the __________ .
7 Ich liebe Toast mit **Schinken** und Käse.	I love toast with ____________ and cheese.
8 Was für ein schönes Geschenk! **Das wäre doch nicht nötig gewesen.**	What a nice present! ______________ ______________ .
9 Stell bitte die Milch in den **Kühlschrank**.	Please put the milk in the ____________ .
10 In der Weihnachtszeit essen wir **Lebkuchen**.	We eat ______________ at Christmas time.
11 Das **Herz** ist das Symbol der Liebe.	The ______________ is the symbol for love.
12 **Alles Liebe / Liebe Grüße**	______________
13 Bist du müde? – Ja, **ein bisschen.**	Are you tired? – Yes, ______________ .
14 Meine Tante **erwartet** ihr erstes Kind.	My aunt is ______________ her first child.

3 Word snail

Übersetze die Wörter ins Englische. Trage die englischen Wörter in die Wortschnecke ein. Die Anfangsbuchstaben in der Schnecke helfen dir. Das Lösungswort findest du in den grauen Feldern.

Lösungswort: ______________________

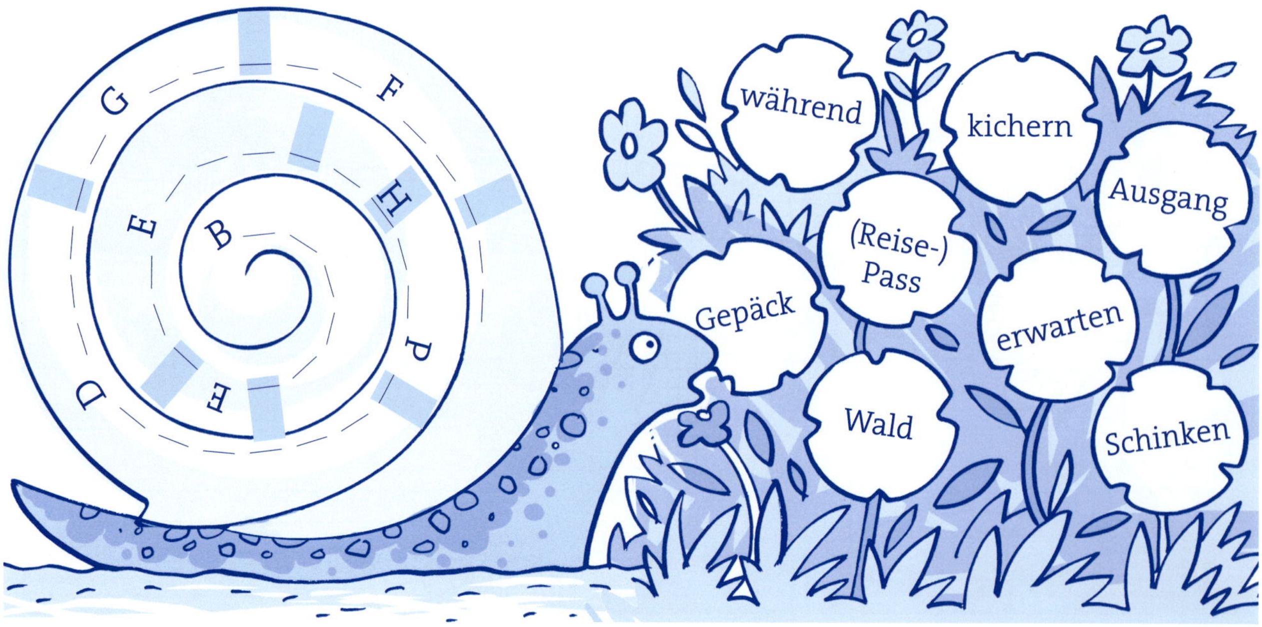

New words ▸ *p. 97 | VOCABULARY p. 218*

1 Ich sah das kaputte Auto meines Bruders und kriegte einen **Schock**.	I saw my brother's damaged car and had a ______________________.
2 **Dreh dich um** und schlaf wieder ein.	______________________ and go back to sleep.
3 Hier gibt es nur eine **Dusche** für 10 Leute.	There's only one ______________ for 10 people.
4 **Endlich** zu Hause!	At home ______________________________!
5 Darf ich dir Tom **vorstellen**?	May I ________________________ you to Tom?
6 **Melde dich**, wenn du etwas sagen möchtest.	____________________________ if you want to say something.
7 Ich möchte dich nicht **küssen**.	I don't want to _______________________ you.
8 Ich stolperte und fiel auf den **Po**.	I stumbled and fell on my _________________.
9 Viele Leute lachen über mich, aber **es macht mir nichts aus**.	A lot of people laugh about me, but __________ ______________________________________.
10 Ich mag Katharina, weil **sie Spaß verträgt**.	I like Katharina because __________________.
11 **Eigentlich** esse ich kein Fleisch.	__________________________, I don't eat meat.

4 Bits and pieces

Verbinde die Silben mit der passenden Vorsilbe und schreibe die Wörter dann in die richtige Spalte.

-change	-side	-healthy	-pect	-portant	-usual	-pensive	-dependent
-prove	-fit	-patient	-troduce	-cuse	-friendly	-perience	-stall
-comfortable	-well	-cluding	-cluded	-cluded	-cluding	-able	-fair

ex-	im-	un-	in-

New words ▸ *p. 98 | VOCABULARY pp. 218–219*

1 Ich **liege** oft auf meinem Bett und höre Musik.	I often __________ on my bed and listen to music.
2 Was ist in dem roten **Topf** auf dem **Herd**?	What's in the red __________ on the __________?
3 Ich war **schockiert**, als ich hörte, dass er tot war.	I was __________ when I heard that he was dead.
4 Ein Brot mit Käse und **Tomaten**, bitte. Tut mir leid, wir haben keine **Tomaten** mehr.	A cheese and __________ sandwich, please. I'm afraid we've run out of __________.
5 Englische Kinder mögen **Bohnen** auf Toast.	English children like __________ on toast.
6 Ich habe keinen **Appetit** heute Abend.	I have no __________ tonight.
7 **Eine Diskothek für Minderjährige** ist eine gute Idee, weil junge Leute dort keinen **Alkohol** kaufen können.	__________ is a good idea because young people can't buy __________ there.
8 **Mach dich fein**, wir gehen aus.	__________, we're going out.
9 **Hochhackige Schuhe** tun weh!	__________ hurt!
10 Hör auf, **Nägel** zu kauen.	Stop biting your __________.

5 Word partners

Verbinde die richtigen Partner, schreibe sie in die Liste und übersetze sie ins Deutsche.

1 high	anthem	__________
2 host	wipers	__________
3 dining	desk	__________
4 tourist	connection	__________
5 driving	heels	__________
6 baggage	office	__________
7 national	room	__________
8 information	licence	__________
9 windscreen	reclaim	__________
10 flight	family	__________

New words ▸ *p. 99 | VOCABULARY p. 219*

1 **Fußgänger** sollten die Straße nur an der Ampel überqueren.	________ should only cross the street at the traffic lights.
2 In Großstädten sieht man viele Straßen**künstler** und Straßen**musikanten**.	You can see lots of street ________ and ________ in big cities.
3 Wir **bestellten Kabeljau** und Pommes frites.	We ________ and chips.
4 Mein englischer Freund schüttete sich viel **Salz** und **Essig** auf seine Pommes frites.	My English friend put lots of ________ and ________ on his chips.
5 Meine Gastmutter nannte mich „**Liebes**“.	My host mother called me “________”.
6 Was für ein **hübsches** Kleid!	What a ________ dress!
7 Das ist zu viel Majonäse! – Igitt!	That's too much ________! – ________!
8 Ich **wette**, du kannst das nicht aufessen.	I ________ you can't finish that.
9 **Ich kann es kaum erwarten**, 18 zu werden.	________ to be 18.

New words ▸ *p. 100 | VOCABULARY pp. 219–220*

1 **Mama** *(irisches Englisch)*	________
2 Wir haben ein Problem mit unseren Fahrkarten, aber Frau Meyer wird es **prüfen**.	We're having a problem with our tickets, but Ms Meyer is going to ________ it.
3 Wir haben einen **seltsamen** Film geguckt.	We watched a ________ film.
4 **Spinat** ist ein grünes Gemüse.	________ is a green vegetable.
5 Ich mag **Curry**wurst.	I like ________ sausage.
6 **Grüß sie von mir.**	________
7 Wir haben an jedem **Wochentag** geöffnet.	We're open every ________.
8 Normalerweise vermeide ich touristische **Orte**.	I usually avoid tourist ________.

6 Linking

Verbinde die passenden Sätze.

1 I like our new English teacher.

2 I often have to look after my little brother, but ...

3 This box is for you. It's my birthday present.

4 ... Write back soon.

5 Who wants to go on a school trip next year?

A Lots of love, John

B You shouldn't have.

C Put up your hands, please.

D She can take a joke.

E I don't mind.

New words ▸ *pp. 102–103 | VOCABULARY p. 220*

1 Mein Bruder sagt, Schweine können fliegen, aber das ist **Unsinn**.	My brother says pigs can fly, but that's ______________________.
2 Tim **widerspricht** mir immer.	Tim always ______________ with me.
3 **Fuß / Füße**	______________________
4 Dublin Castle können Sie **zu Fuß** erreichen.	You can get to Dublin Castle __________.
5 Dublins Kathedrale **wurde** vor über 800 Jahren **gebaut**.	Dublin's cathedral ______________ over 800 years ago.

7 Scrambled sentences

Bringe die Wörter in die richtige Reihenfolge.

1 a language / a great / Going on / to learn / an exchange / is / way

____.

2 culture / also learn / about / You will / a lot / another

____.

3 people / and English / Some / Irish / Irish / speak

____.

4 of history / Dublin / lots / with / is / Ireland's capital

____.

8 Word snail

Finde acht englische Verben in der Schnecke. Kreise sie ein und schreibe die deutsche Übersetzung in die Liste.

1 ______________________ 5 ______________________

2 ______________________ 6 ______________________

3 ______________________ 7 ______________________

4 ______________________ 8 ______________________

9 Odd word out

Unterstreiche das Wort, das nicht in die Reihe passt, und finde einen Oberbegriff für die anderen drei Wörter.

head – heart – bottom – <u>pride</u> parts of the body

1 train – plane – cruise – boat ______________________

2 hundred – number – thousand – ten ______________________

3 palace – flat – cottage – baggage ______________________

4 juice – coffee – alcohol – salt ______________________

5 marzipan – ketchup – vinegar – mayonnaise ______________________

10 Spot the mistakes

In jedem Satz sind zwei Fehler. Unterstreiche und korrigiere sie.

1 My dad is a funtastic cooker. ______________________

2 Your next connexion is flight Nr. AB 15. ______________________

3 Can I take a shauer? – Actualy, no. ______________________

11 Crossword

Hier kannst du testen, wie gut du die Vokabeln aus dem Band 3 behalten hast.

1 someone who leaves his own country to live in another country
2 a new or difficult thing you haven't done before
3 → a big bedroom in a hostel
3 ↓ ◂▸clean
4 someone who sells things
5 simple past of „run“
6 the landing of a plane
7 Keep your dog on a ???!
8 a black and yellow insect
9 where adults meet to drink alcohol
10 where no. 26 lives

11 the leaving of a plane
12 simple past of "lie"
13 run fast behind someone in order to catch him or her
14 people can fly in it
15 what a chicken lays
16 a high building
17 where you can buy bread and cake
18 → someone's female child
18 ↓ ◂▸ alive
19 a very brave person
20 part of a school year
21 to try something in your mouth
22 to give lessons

23 a small track
24 → under
24 ↓ next to
25 the continent we live on
26 the most important female of a royal family
27 where you collect your baggage from at the airport
28 to touch someone with your lips
29 ◂▸ sell
30 something very bad or sad
31 what Londoners call their underground
32 land outside towns

G

3

HEADLIGHT

Wordmaster
Lösungen

Cornelsen

Unit 1: I love London

New words pp. 8–9
1 palace; queen 2 prime minister 3 stadium 4 bells 5 towers 6 Europe 7 carnival 8 detective 9 the Tube 10 underground 11 ride 12 takes 13 speech 14 's; called 15 Parliament; sights

1 Lost words
1 at 2 on 3 for 4 in 5 on 6 in 7 for 8 at; at 9 to

New words p. 10
1 local 2 by 3 reporter 4 I've lived here all my life. 5 not anywhere 6 things to do 7 downside; upside 8 is able to help

New words pp. 10–11
1 dirty 2 fashion 3 (shopping) mall 4 shop 5 is allowed to go 6 cultures 7 Greek; Irish; Scottish 8 huge 9 crowded; traffic

2 Word pairs
Scottish Irish Greek

3 Crossword

		1 P											
		A						2 F		3 H			
4 B	E	L	L		5 D			A		U			
		A			E			6 S	I	G	H	7 T	S
	8 S	C	O	T	T	I	S	H		E		O	
9 D		E			E			I				W	
I					C			O				E	
R					T			N				R	
10 T	R	A	F	F	I	C							
Y					V								
			11 Q	U	E	E	N						

4 Odd word out
1 famous 2 traffic 3 fashion 4 detective 5 Greek 6 boat

5 Spot the mistakes
1 Queen; Palace 2 famous; detective 3 special; underground 4 visit; Parliament 5 There; on

New words pp. 12–13
1 book 2 Travelcard 3 just 4 stall 5 Olympics 6 high street 7 over 8 discuss 9 Write down 10 captions 11 present 12 heading

New words pp. 14–16
1 contact 2 off; path 3 Click (on) booking 4 comments 5 frequent 6 (tour) guide; route 7 No way! 8 rest 9 youth 10 loud 11 pay for 12 escalators 13 airport 14 arrival 15 departure gate 16 flight 17 plane 18 check-in; check in

6 What are the words: *think – think of – think about*
1 think of/about 2 think about 3 think 4 think of/about 5 think 6 think of

7 Bits and pieces
1 underground = U-Bahn
2 downside = Kehrseite, Nachteil
3 traffic = Verkehr
4 fashion = Mode
5 upside = gute Seite, Vorteil
6 transport = Verkehrsmittel; Transport(wesen)
7 check-in = Check-in; Einchecken
8 escalator = Rolltreppe

8 Word building
1 Rede, Ansprache; reden, sprechen
2 Reporter/in; berichten
3 Geschäft, Laden; einkaufen
4 Buchung; buchen
5 Diskussion; diskutieren
6 Präsentation; präsentieren

New words p. 17
1 a big deal 2 solve 3 Natural History 4 dinosaur 5 rolled 6 like this 7 plan 8 Take it easy. 9 change 10 get on 11 eastbound 12 Line

9 Opposites
1 huge 2 departure 3 downside 4 everywhere 5 dirty 6 excited/nervous 7 over 8 youth 9 quiet 10 eastbound

New words pp. 18–19
1 sell 2 typical 3 around 4 million 5 calm 6 touch 7 private 8 dead 9 guard 10 Catch 11 point of view

10 The fourth word

1 queen 2 Travelcard 3 plane 4 loud 5 stadium 6 speech 7 palace 8 stalls 9 crowded 10 heading

11 Word snake

		F	L	I	G	H	T							
		A	I	R	P	O	R	T						
A	R	R	I	V	A	L								
C	H	E	C	K	-	I	N							
						D	E	P	A	R	T	U	R	E
				P	L	A	N	E						
				P	A	Y								

New words pp. 20–21

1 course 2 article 3 kilometres per hour (km/h) 4 per 5 hotel; office

New words pp. 22–23

1 Public transport 2 public 3 once 4 Central 5 zone 6 tonight 7 circus 8 embankment 9 Cathedral 10 ringtone

12 Word search

A	S	L	P	A	I	D
R	B	E	T	S	P	M
L	E	F	H	T	F	E
Z	G	T	O	O	K	A
S	A	M	U	O	T	N
A	N	G	G	D	E	T
W	H	Y	H	R	E	W
T	O	G	T	E	U	I

	Infinitive	simple past	past participle
1	pay	paid	paid
2	begin	began	begun
3	think	thought	thought
4	stand	stood	stood
5	fight	fought	fought
6	mean	meant	meant
7	take	took	taken
8	get	got	got
9	leave	left	left
10	see	saw	seen

13 Do you remember?

P	S	F	I	R	E		S	T	A	T	I	O	N	H	S
O	U	T	B	U	A	I	R	P	O	R	T	A	O	B	H
S	P	U	U	N	Q	A	B	W	C	C	D	S	E	F	O
T	E	B	S	D	U	G	E	H	A	I	P	A	R	K	P
	R	E		E	A	R	B	F	J	I	K	L	M	N	P
O	M	M	S	R	R	S	E	R	T	A	E	H	T	O	I
F	A	U	T	G	I	C	P	A	I	Q	T	R	A	I	N
F	R	I	O	R	U	H	L	R	S	D	S	H	O	P	G
I	K	D	P	O	M	O	T	U	V	W	G	X	Y	Z	
C	E	A	Z	U	A	O	B	C	D	M	U	E	S	U	M
E	T	T	O	N	E	L	F	G	H	C	I	N	E	M	A
I	J	S	O	D	T	A	X	I	P	A	L	A	C	E	L
K	L	M	S	W	I	M	M	I	N	G		P	O	O	L
M	A	R	K	E	T	T	N	A	R	U	A	T	S	E	R
N	S	H	O	P	P	I	N	G		C	E	N	T	R	E

Sights: museum, theatre, palace, stadium, bridge, tower
Other places: hospital, fire station
Traffic/Transport: bus stop, taxi, Tube, underground, airport, train
Where you can have fun: cafe, restaurant, cinema, school, park, aquarium, zoo, swimming pool
Where you can buy things: shopping mall, shop, shopping centre, post office, supermarket, market

Unit 2: Country life

New words pp. 29–31
1 farmhouse 2 tractor 3 traditional 4 Nowhere 5 in the middle of nowhere 6 try to be 7 business 8 start a business 9 van 10 install; CCTV camera 11 It sucks! 12 or something 13 sounds 14 keep 15 Keep me posted! 16 pain 17 What a pain! 18 lead

1 What's the word: *anywhere, everywhere* or *nowhere*?
1 everywhere 2 everywhere; anywhere 3 Nowhere 4 anywhere

New words p. 32
1 hero 2 brave; deep 3 drown 4 heavy 5 save 6 react 7 do a great job 8 chase 9 recently 10 recent 11 PC 12 respect 13 respect 14 countryside 15 anything

New words p. 33
1 take a message 2 leave a message 3 This is 4 speak to 5 I'm afraid; right now 6 the other day 7 son

2 Numbers and letters
nowhere shop church business van install cameras sucks lead chase millions

Lösungssatz: *Keep me posted!*

New words pp. 34–36
1 ever 2 Have you ever been to 3 move house 4 twice 5 results 6 for two months 7 since August 8 engineers 9 farmers; after 10 pub 11 track 12 wood 13 diagram 14 cycle 15 tour 16 crossroads

3 Picture puzzle
1 van 2 CCTV camera 3 gate 4 tractor 5 plane

4 Word snail
heavy countryside drown brave crossroads twice hero engineer

Lösungswort: *tractor*

5 Linking
1 It sucks! = Es nervt! / Es ist Mist!
2 CCTV camera = Überwachungskamera
3 Keep me posted. = Halt mich auf dem Laufenden.
4 What a pain! = So ein Mist. / Es nervt!
5 Take it easy. = Reg dich nicht auf! / Bleib mal locker!
6 take a message = (jm.) etwas ausrichten, eine Nachricht annehmen
7 leave a message = eine Nachricht hinterlassen
8 the other day = neulich
9 be called = heißen
10 move house = umziehen

6 Plurals
1 businesses 2 heroes 3 points of view 4 children 5 cultures 6 high streets 7 downsides 8 upsides

7 Find the right word: *since* or *for*?
1 since 2 since 3 for 4 Since 5 For

New words p. 37
1 city slicker 2 country bumpkin 3 over; fence 4 hole 5 beside 6 laughed at 7 princess; prince 8 drove 9 is good with 10 blushed 11 trains; sheepdogs 12 bush 13 dump; dump

8 Definitions
1 pub 2 twice 3 crossroads 4 wood 5 fence 6 CCTV camera

New words p. 38
1 illegal 2 dumper 3 suggest 4 Offer 5 farmyard 6 yard 7 jumped; bat 8 impatient 9 patient

9 Word ladder
1 fine 2 find 3 kind 4 king 5 ring 6 sing 7 song 8 long

New words p. 39
1 knocked on 2 Police officers 3 disturb 4 watch for 5 park; resident

10 Word families
1 sound = klingen; sound = Geräusch, Klang, Laut
2 ride = reiten; ride = Fahrt; Fahrgeschäft
3 respect = respektieren, achten; respect = Respekt
4 depart = abfahren, abfliegen; departure = Abfahrt, Abflug
5 fly = fliegen; flight = Flug

6 dump = abladen; dump = (Müll-)Abladeplatz; Deponie
7 discuss = diskutieren; discussion = Diskussion
8 mean = bedeuten, meinen; meaning = Bedeutung
9 react = reagieren; reaction = Reaktion
10 suggest = etwas vorschlagen; suggestion = Vorschlag
11 book = buchen; booking = Buchung
12 sell = verkaufen; sale = Verkauf

New words pp. 40–41
1 foreground; background 2 detail 3 structure 4 brilliant 5 reason 6 for lots of reasons; Firstly; secondly; thirdly 7 independent from 8 ideal 9 paragraph; general; statement

11 Word snake

	Infinitive	Simple past	Past participle
1	write	wrote	written
2	take	took	taken
3	pay	paid	paid
4	catch	caught	caught
5	fly	flew	flown
6	sell	sold	sold
7	drive	drove	driven
8	keep	kept	kept

New words pp. 42–43
1 notice 2 grandad 3 character 4 episode

12 Do you remember?

A	B	X	C	G	R	A	N	D	M	A
I	Z	S	O	N	C	O	U	S	I	N
G	G	T	U	N	C	L	E	M	O	G
B	R	D	S	I	S	T	E	R	S	R
R	A	A	I	J	T	X	Q	T	T	A
O	N	U	N	Z	E	W	S	J	E	N
T	D	G	N	D	P	H	A	C	P	D
H	M	H	M	U	F	O	U	F	M	A
E	O	T	O	S	A	A	N	A	O	D
R	T	E	T	A	T	U	T	T	T	O
J	H	R	H	F	H	I	L	H	H	P
F	E	H	E	Z	E	M	M	E	E	X
S	R	G	R	I	R	Z	Y	R	R	R

1 grandfather, grandmother
2 grandma, grandad
3 cousin, cousin
4 son, daughter
5 uncle, aunt
6 sister, brother
7 stepmother, stepfather
8 mother, father

Unit 3: Liverpool … the world in one city

New words pp. 50–51
1 entry 2 disaster 3 Chinese 4 Name 5 migrants 6 port 7 Slavery 8 international 9 fool

1 Words with a different meaning
1 need 2 message 3 drive 4 save 5 jump

New words pp. 52–53
1 dumb 2 policy 3 confectionery 4 More and more 5 suspends 6 confiscates 7 Yours sincerely

2 Lost words
1 about 2 at 3 from 4 from 5 in 6 at; at 7 of 8 from 9 about

New words pp. 54–55
1 talent 2 business studies 3 term 4 salesperson 5 serious 6 is taking part in; competition 7 is good at 8 challenge 9 Business people 10 products 11 get started 12 make money 13 profit 14 film 15 grand final 16 cost 17 presentation 18 euros 19 badge; balloon

3 Word building

Noun	entry	beginning	sale	plan	rest
Verb	enter	begin	sell	plan	rest

Noun	tradition	dirt	nation
Adjective	traditional	dirty	national

Noun	independence	challenge
Adjective	independent	challenging

1 entry 2 rest 3 enter 4 dirty 5 sell 6 national

New words pp. 56–58

1 lend 2 coconut; tarts; taste 3 bakery 4 make a decision 5 cookies; ourselves 6 rice; menu 7 Bees 8 ice 9 mouse; mice 10 cucumbers

4 Word partners

1 airport = Flughafen
2 international = international
3 slavery = Sklaverei
4 ringtone = Klingelton
5 countryside = Landschaft, Umgebung, Natur
6 crossroads = (Straßen-)Kreuzung
7 foreground = Vordergrund
8 background = Hintergrund
9 paragraph = Absatz
10 salesperson = Verkäufer/in

5 Do you remember?

E	G	G	A	C	H	E	E	S	E	B	X	Y	F
C	Y	O	G	U	R	T	C	O	O	K	I	E	L
O	Q	M	L	C	H	O	C	O	L	A	T	E	O
C	P	E	B	U	T	T	E	R	S	N	Y	C	U
O	O	L	M	M	K	J	A	M	R	A	C	A	R
N	T	E	P	B	R	E	A	D	E	N	N	R	N
U	A	T	F	E	G	N	A	R	O	A	U	R	G
T	T	T	J	R	Y	T	S	A	P	K	T	O	C
B	O	E	Z	A	H	C	F	P	P	A	S	T	A
C	O	C	O	A	M	I	L	K	V	X	M	O	K
E	C	O	F	F	E	E	L	A	S	A	G	N	E

Fruits and vegetables: cucumber, apple, carrot, potato, nuts, orange, coconut
Things we get from animals: egg, milk, meat
Things we make, cook or bake: yogurt, cheese, chocolate, flour, bread, butter, cake, cocoa, cookie, coffee, jam, lasagne, omelette, pasta, pasty

New words pp. 59–61

1 dance 2 mix 3 flour 4 broke 5 broken 6 eggs 7 floor 8 almonds 9 It's a money-saver 10 cross with 11 China 12 complain about 13 successful 14 needs to 15 label; Goodies 16 test 17 want Tim to come 18 throw

6 Word web

1 plate 2 fence 3 plane 4 mouse 5 apple 6 prize 7 smile

7 Find the right word: *lend* or *borrow*

1 borrow 2 lend 3 borrow 4 lent 5 borrow 6 borrowed

New words p. 62

1 sportswoman 2 as 3 box 4 female 5 the Olympics 6 medals 7 role model 8 strong; weak 9 gym 10 mark

8 The fourth word

1 article 2 difficult 3 nowhere 4 son 5 ride 6 impatient 7 episode 8 confectionery

New words p. 63

1 opinion 2 hard-working 3 skinny 4 sum up; message 5 summarize 6 On the one hand; on the other hand 7 definite 8 definitely 9 even 10 violent 11 take up 12 beginning

9 Opposites

1 beginning 2 sell 3 less and less 4 be good at sth. 5 daugther 6 under 7 impatient 8 strong 9 international 10 grandad

New words pp. 64–65

1 tourist office 2 mention 3 pass the ball! 4 beat 5 shot 6 Hard luck! 7 summary 8 Skipping; pilates

10 Word families

Noun	comment	name	notice	dump
Verb	comment	name	notice	dump

Noun	summary
Verb	summarize

Noun	discovery	product	bicycle	film
Verb	discover	produce	cycle	film

Noun	answer
Verb	answer

Manchmal haben englische Verben und Nomen *dieselbe* Form.

1 summarize 2 answer 3 dump 4 discover 5 cycle

11 Crossword

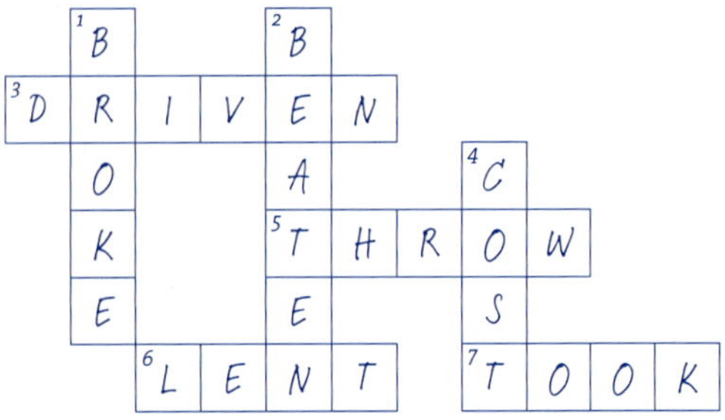

1 broke 2 beaten 3 driven 4 cost 5 throw
6 lent 7 took

12 Word pairs

get started	take sth. up
make money	be good with
take part (in)	be good at
sum sth. up	make a decision

Unit 4: Bonnie Scotland

New words pp. 70–71

1 bonnie 2 Scotland; the United Kingdom/the UK
3 the Highlands 4 capital 5 enemy 6 symbol

1 Scrambled words

capital cheese castle cucumber control charity comment children cupcake complain countryside competition

Lösung: *the United Kingdom*

New words pp. 72–73

1 change 2 close down 3 equipment 4 out-of-town 5 manager 6 In all; employees
7 unemployed 8 blame 9 stick together
10 themselves 11 bed and breakfast (B & B)
12 how to run a business 13 teaches 14 Help yourselves. 15 store 16 management 17 staff

New words pp. 74–75

1 area 2 welcome 3 bank; fish 4 including
5 take place 6 twin room 7 dry; coat 8 serve
9 dining room 10 a 16-year-old 11 telephone
12 confirm; reservation 13 guest; Canadian
14 ring 15 knife; knives 16 dish 17 bananas

2 Find the right words

1 herself 2 ourselves 3 himself 4 itself
5 myself 6 themselves 7 yourselves 8 yourself

3 Word ladder

1 cost 2 coat 3 boat 4 beat 5 meat 6 meal
7 deal 8 dear 9 hear 10 gear

New words pp. 76–78

1 Boil 2 Scots 3 kettle 4 waiters; waitresses
5 mechanic 6 receptionist 7 charge

New words p. 79

1 add 2 clues 3 land 4 hire 5 driving licence
6 onto; hooted 7 Luckily 8 stressed

4 Numbers and letters

changes Highlands ago store close down customers both unemployed started bed and breakfast stick together runs shopping guest capital welcomed

Lösungssatz: *Come and stay with us this summer!*

5 Word friends

palace: princess, king
capital: Berlin, London
enemy: bad, dangerous
store: buy, shop
equipment: tent, sleeping bag
staff: employee, worker

New words p. 80

1 narrow 2 winding; bends 3 windscreen wipers
4 signal 5 building 6 accent 7 wonder
8 haunted 9 such a 10 There is no such thing as
11 ghost 12 Canada

6 Word families

	Verb	German
1	change	1 sich umziehen / 2 umsteigen
2	employ	beschäftigen
3	start	beginnen, anfangen
4	store	lagern
5	confirm	bestätigen
6	reserve	reservieren, buchen

	Noun	German
1	change	Veränderung, Wechsel
2	employee	Arbeitnehmer/in
3	start	Anfang, Start
4	store	Geschäft, Laden
5	confirmation	Bestätigung
6	reservation	Reservierung, Buchung

New words p. 81
1 midnight 2 shone 3 bagpipes 4 wall
5 puzzled 6 fingers 7 side 8 I think so. 9 I don't think so.

7 Find the right words: time words
today last week this Saturday Tonight yesterday
the night before tomorrow

8 Opposites
1 unemployed 2 enemy 3 start 4 empty
5 I don't think so.

9 Plurals
1 mice 2 16-year-olds 3 policies 4 twin rooms
5 employees 6 driving licences 7 waitresses
8 knives 9 enemies 10 heroes

New words pp. 82–83
1 Imagine 2 travel 3 national anthem 4 God save the Queen. 5 pride 6 move 7 thousand

10 Definitions
1 charge 2 egg 3 pasta 4 recently 5 ring
6 serve 7 waiter 8 guest 9 capital 10 employee
11 enemy

Lösungswort: *reservation*

11 Word building
1 change 2 employee; employed 3 puzzled
4 teach 5 building 6 pride

New words pp. 84–85
1 Skim; bold 2 a couple of 3 somewhere
4 accommodation 5 stay 6 dormitories 7 meal
8 Perhaps

12 Find the right words

	Infinitive	Simple past	Past participle
1	teach	taught	taught
2	shine	shone	shone
3	run a hotel	ran	run
4	stick together	stuck together	stuck together
5	ring	rang	rung
6	take	took	taken
7	write	wrote	written
8	pay	paid	paid
9	sell	sold	sold
10	catch	caught	caught

13 Word search

I	N	D	E	P	E	N	D	E	N	T	O	R	C	H	E
C	O	N	F	I	R	M	S	L	A	V	E	R	Y	Q	E
O	L	A	T	I	P	A	C	L	Y	U	A	C	U	G	M
A	K	N	I	F	E	M	A	B	C	M	R	I	U	V	P
T	B	A	N	A	N	A	T	M	A	O	P	H	D	S	L
C	S	E	R	I	O	U	S	Z	S	M	H	D	E	T	O
M	O	E	L	T	T	E	K	S	E	N	T	N	I	O	Y
W	B	U	O	B	I	N	R	N	D	O	U	I	C	R	E
B	A	T	N	H	G	O	T	H	W	L	C	B	E	E	E
A	B	S	G	T	A	B	R	E	T	S	A	S	I	D	K
O	L	O	M	D	R	I	R	O	T	A	L	A	C	S	E
N	Y	H	S	D	O	Y	T	A	T	O	M	I	G	E	N
T	D	G	E	Y	R	G	S	R	V	S	T	E	U	M	E
P	O	S	S	I	B	L	E	I	A	E	S	T	E	X	M
C	H	A	L	L	E	N	G	E	D	M	M	J	S	T	Y
S	H	O	T	I	M	P	A	T	I	E	N	T	T	Y	B

Unit 5: A stay in Dublin

New words pp. 92–93
1 exchange 2 improve 3 experience 4 prefer, to 5 probably 6 get to know 7 might 8 partly 9 likes; dislikes

1 Word web
1 ghost 2 heart 3 sight 4 guest 5 start 6 fight 7 point

New words pp. 94–95
1 No./no. 2 belt 3 EU (= European Union) 4 Non- 5 flight connection 6 baggage; baggage reclaim 7 exit 8 during 9 passport 10 hosts 11 unusual 12 usual 13 Anyway

2 Find the right words: at the airport
1 arrival 2 departure 3 baggage reclaim 4 plane 5 baggage 6 passport 7 ticket 8 information desk 9 belt

New words p. 96
1 line 2 shook, hand; giggled 3 count 4 rude 5 marzipan 6 forest 7 ham 8 You shouldn't have 9 fridge 10 gingerbread 11 heart 12 Lots of love 13 a little 14 expecting

3 Word snail
baggage – exit – expect – ham – passport – during – giggle – forest

Lösungswort: *exchange*

New words p. 97
1 shock 2 Turn over 3 shower 4 at last 5 introduce 6 Put up your hand 7 kiss 8 bottom 9 I don't mind 10 she can take a joke 11 Actually

4 Bits and pieces
exchange, expect, experience, expensive, excuse, excluding, excluded

improve, impatient, important

unusual, unfriendly, unhealthy, unfit, uncomfortable, unwell, unable, unfair

introduce, inside, install, independent, including, included

New words p. 98
1 lie 2 pot; cooker 3 shocked 4 tomato; tomatoes 5 beans 6 appetite 7 An underage disco; alcohol 8 Get dressed up 9 High heels 10 nails

5 Word partners
1 high heels = hochhackige Schuhe
2 host family = Gastfamilie
3 dining room = Esszimmer
4 tourist office = Touristeninformation, Fremdenverkehrsbüro
5 driving licence = Führerschein
6 baggage reclaim = Gepäckausgabe
7 national anthem = Nationalhymne
8 information desk = Informationsschalter
9 windscreeen wipers = Scheibenwischer
10 flight connection = Anschlussflug

New words p. 99
1 Pedestrians 2 artists; buskers 3 ordered; cod 4 salt; vinegar 5 love 6 pretty 7 mayonnaise; Yuck! 8 bet 9 I can't wait

New words p. 100
1 mam 2 look into 3 weird 4 Spinach 5 curry 6 Give her my love. 7 weekday 8 sites

6 Linking
1 D 2 E 3 B 4 A 5 C

New words p. 102–103
1 rubbish 2 disagrees 3 foot; feet 4 on foot 5 was built

7 Scrambled sentences
1 Going on an exchange is a great way to learn a language.
2 You will also learn a lot about another culture.
3 Some Irish people speak Irish and English.
4 Dublin is Ireland's capital with lots of history.

8 Word snail
1 zählen 2 verbessern 3 küssen 4 vorstellen 5 schütteln 6 bestellen 7 erwarten 8 liegen

9 Odd word out
1 cruise; ways to travel 2 number; number words 3 baggage; buildings 4 salt; things you can drink 5 marzipan; you put it on chips

10 Spot the mistakes

1 fantastic, cook 2 connection, No. 3 shower, Actually

11 Crossword

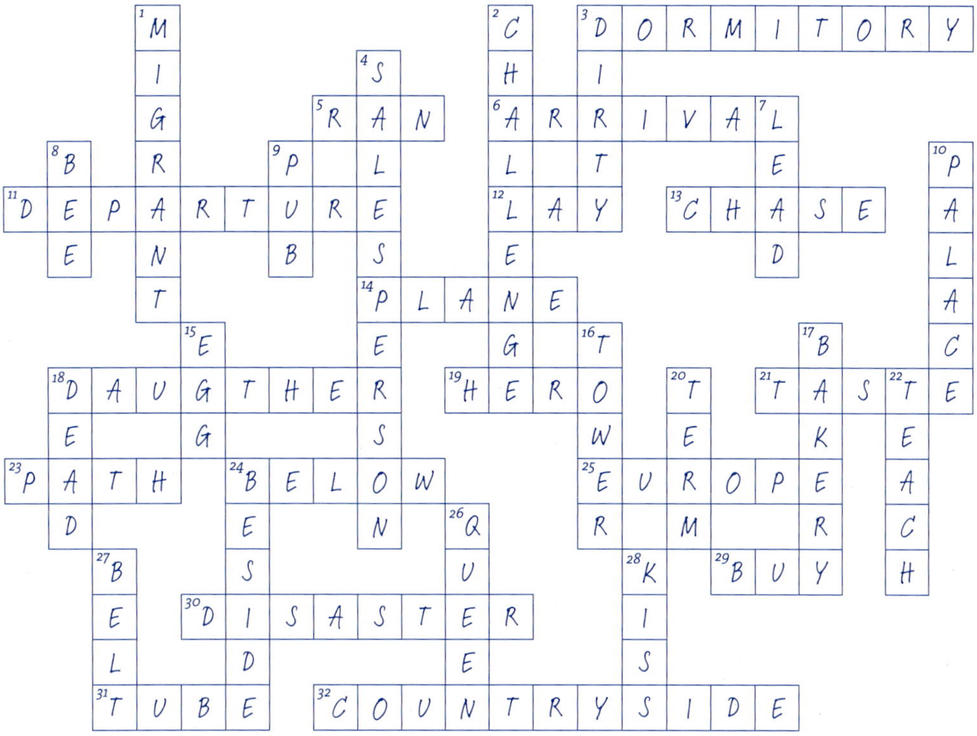